"This volunteer-led affinity concept is the most effectual cultivation and prospect-qualification model I've encountered in twenty years. I have never seen a group of volunteers and prospects so eager for further involvement. I recommend it all the time."
—**Henry D. Lewis, president, Development Consultant Associates**

"The immediate impact on our volunteers was a revelation to me. Their relationship to the cause became richer, their advocacy skills grew stronger, and the horizons for their personal gift-planning expanded."
—**Laura Breeze, director of development, Sarasota Opera**

"We have been using the author's effective affinity model for eight years. It has enabled us to identify 'millionaires next door' and to motivate them to act upon their love for our college."
—**Dr. C. Ben Wright, vice president of institutional advancement, Dunwoody Institute**

"A must-read for any organization—whether large or small, new or old—that needs to dramatically increase its fundraising revenues."
—**James A. Keenan, Jr., president, Keenan Associates**

"This process just makes good common sense, common sense the rest of us never thought about before the authors introduced it to us."
—**Susan Freeman, executive director, Volunteers Enlisted to Assist People (VEAP)**

"Our board and volunteers were new to development. The interviews were a great chance not only to warm them up for personal calls, but also to get us to know our very good friends who love the library and are willing to contribute if you only knock on their door!"
—**Inez Bergquist, president, Waltman Associates**

"This book is mandatory reading for the one-person shop but I have also observed the authors' process successfully implemented in diverse settings: inner city youth, scouting, senior care, colleges, faith communities, a seminary, and a library. I myself have used the program successfully in a major arts organization and a large city hospital."
—**Nancy Slaughter, community volunteer**

The Jossey-Bass Nonprofit & Public Management Series also includes:

Hidden Assets

Revolutionize
Your Development
Program with a
Volunteer-Driven
Approach

Diane L. Hodiak
John S. Ryan

JOSSEY-BASS
A Wiley Company
San Francisco

Jossey-Bass books and products are available through most bookstores. To contact Jossey-Bass directly, call (888) 378-2537, fax to (800) 605-2665, or visit our website at www.josseybass.com.
Substantial discounts on bulk quantities of Jossey-Bass books are available to corporations, professional associations, and other organizations. For details and discount information, contact the special sales department at Jossey-Bass.

Library of Congress Cataloging-in-Publication Data

Hodiak, Diane L.
   Hidden assets: revolutionize your development program with a volunteer-driven approach / Diane L. Hodiak, John S. Ryan.—1st ed. p. cm.—(The Jossey-Bass nonprofit and public management series)
   ISBN 0-7879-5351-2 (alk. paper)
   1. Fund raising. 2. Nonprofit organizations—Finance. 3. Voluntarism. I. Ryan, John S., date. II. Title. III. Series.

HV41.2 .H63 2001
658.15"224—dc21   00-011523

FIRST EDITION

PB Printing   10 9 8 7 6 5 4 3 2 1

Contents

102594

Tables, Figures, Exhibits, and Worksheets

Worksheets

Preface

THIS BOOK is based on more than 2,500 interviews. Most were conducted by volunteers; the interviewees had been evaluated and rated as among the very best prospects. Here's a sample of what the interviewers found:

- A social worker for a retirement center secures a $250,000 gift from an elderly resident who wants to express his gratitude to the staff. In addition to the staff support fund, the same resident later makes an estate gift in the six-figure range.

- During a personal visit, an elderly couple indicates that they plan to donate their entire estate to the charity. Over the next fifteen years they make gifts of $3 million. They leave an additional $14 million in their estate.

- A national charity implements the affinity fundraising program and interviews 1,200 active members. They discover that 40 percent of those interviewed will make some type of planned gift to the organization.

- The chief fundraising officer from a technical school has continued to successfully use affinity fundraising for more than eight years. It has been used as part of the ongoing development program, including their most recent accomplishment—the multi-million-dollar campaign.

You will learn how your organization can achieve similar results.

• • •

Without question, the philanthropist is everywhere, not just living in the wealthiest neighborhoods and displaying an affluent lifestyle. Every charity has donors, staff, and volunteers who care deeply about the organization. Affinity fundraising will help you discover and build a lifelong relationship with these individuals. They are your hidden assets. Harness their time, interest, and generosity, and you will open the door to incredible wealth.

Affinity fundraising is simple. It does not require technical training. Whether your organization concerns itself with arts, human services, faith, education, environment, politics, or advocacy, the principles remain the same. They apply to new as well as to more mature organizations. This book will help development managers, board members, volunteers, and executives learn through easy, step-by-step techniques how to raise more money than they ever imagined possible.

We believe that once you understand affinity fundraising, it will influence the way you work and think. You will understand why affinity is more important than the appearance of wealth and position. It will help you eliminate the unnecessary and costly steps that are inherent in more traditional fundraising methods. As you eliminate the barriers that have traditionally undermined fundraising, you will learn to enjoy visiting with the individuals who care so much about your organization.

You may be surprised to find out that many volunteers will want to help with the affinity fundraising effort. This is in sharp contrast to more traditional fundraising campaigns in which staff and volunteers may be reluctant to participate initially, then later become overwhelmed or uncomfortable and fail to follow through on their assignments.

You will learn a simple yet monumentally powerful technique that will teach you what to say when you visit with donors. So that you can use your time most effectively, we'll teach you the listening secrets that will help you determine the potential of each individual.

By following these simple steps, you will learn how to help these special individuals understand that they can fulfill their personal philanthropic dreams through a mutual relationship with your organization. Even those of apparently modest means have been known to bequeath their entire estate, often amounting to millions of dollars, to their beloved nonprofit. And many donors desire to donate their money sooner, during their lifetime, so that they can witness the results of their generosity.

There is no need to wait. We will take you down the path today. Learn the shortcuts that will lead your organization to a multi-million-dollar treasure chest. Regardless of the size or nature of your organization, or the sophistication of your current development efforts, you can start to cultivate the individuals who have the greatest affinity for your work and mission.

Best of all, we will show you how to recruit volunteers to help you complete this exciting effort. Working together, you will be able to jump-start your annual giving program, create an endowment program, identify volunteers for a capital campaign, or secure planned gifts in the six- and seven-figure range. This book will show you how to identify your prospects and donors for each of these giving areas, as well as how to guide them through the giving process.

Affinity fundraising is being done across the country, in rural and urban areas, in small towns and larger cities. The nonprofit organizations whose case examples appear in this book have developed ways to tap into the human and financial resources that volunteers offer. You'll read about their successes and learn how to avoid some common pitfalls. You will learn what human resources are necessary for success, as well as how to capitalize on the strengths within your own organization. Read and discover how to adapt these powerful techniques to the unique culture of your organization.

December 2000

Diane L. Hodiak
Seattle, Washington
John S. Ryan
Minneapolis, Minnesota

Acknowledgments

THE AUTHORS wish to thank the many individuals who have made this book possible, including those who may not be mentioned here. We particularly wish to remember the nonprofit visionaries who had the courage and insight to try a new fundraising approach. It is their attitude and conviction that will now make it possible for other nonprofit organizations to benefit. The organizations that continue to practice affinity fundraising and who have shared their stories within should also be commended for their willingness to participate.

We also wish to thank Dorothy Hearst at Jossey-Bass for her support in encouraging the book's development and her colleague, Johanna Vondeling, editor, for her acuity in organization and content.

Special thanks to the reviewers who provided opinions and suggestions early in the manuscript's development. Their encouragement and ideas helped improve the manuscript and make it more usable by its intended audience.

I, Diane L. Hodiak, wish to dedicate this book to John, Danielle, and Joanna. I offer a special remembrance for Hank Rosso, for his inspiration and support.

I, John S. Ryan, wish to dedicate this book to David L. Roberts and Robert J. Odegard of Wheaton College and the University of Minnesota Foundation.
Dave introduced me to affinity fundraising, and Bob gave me a chance to practice it in a major research institution made up of countless smaller charitable causes.

The Authors

DIANE L. HODIAK counsels nonprofit organizations in the start-up and expansion of individual giving programs. She is cofounder of Development Resource Center (drcharity.com), a company that focuses on techniques that offer substantial benefits to nonprofits working with limited resources. As a trainer and counselor, Hodiak seeks to increase the capacity of nonprofit staff and volunteers in fundraising, marketing, planning, and promotion.

Hodiak is coauthor, with Michael Henley, of *Fund Raising and Marketing in the One-Person Shop: Achieving Success with Limited Resources* (2000) and is the author of *The Indispensable Guide to Lists* (1998) and *Publicity: How to Get It for Free or Next to Nothing* (1998).

Hodiak's career experience includes work as a director of public relations and as an executive of three nonprofit organizations. She currently resides in Seattle, Washington, where she volunteers as a board member for two nonprofit organizations.

JOHN S. RYAN entered the field of professional fundraising in 1960. He served as vice president and director of planned giving at the University of Minnesota Foundation (UMF) for ten years, where he created the UMF Planned Giving Department; he trained the staff and coordinated the marketing for large gifts.

Ryan credits his seventeen years as a planned giving officer for Wheaton College in Illinois for providing the experience to teach others how to motivate potential philanthropists to action. He is a Wheaton graduate.

Ryan founded Major Gifts, Inc., in 1987; MGI is entering its fourteenth year of teaching not-for-profits how to identify, recruit, train, and support volunteers in supplementing the work of a development team.

His client list includes Bethel College, Central Lutheran Church, Luther Seminary, Pioneer Retirement Community, Shattuck–St. Mary's School, and the United Hospital Foundation.

Ryan has published twenty-eight articles in professional journals and has been a featured speaker at numerous national conferences. Presently he is chairman of the fund development committee of Suicide Awareness/Voices of Education (SAVE), Minneapolis.

Part One

Understanding the Affinity Approach

Chapter 1

How Volunteers Can Strengthen Donor Relationships

RAISING LARGE SUMS of money may seem like a formidable task, given the limited resources of many organizations. Unfortunately, this situation is often worsened when staff and volunteers have not had positive fundraising experiences; they may be reluctant, at first, to participate.

But fundraising can be an exciting and positive experience for everyone involved. As you will discover when you implement the affinity fundraising model, your volunteers and staff will experience a new sense of reward and accomplishment that will motivate them to continue their involvement. Volunteerism, if properly cultivated, is the path to your hidden assets—your untapped human and financial resources.

This chapter provides you with an overview of affinity fundraising. You will learn its advantages and disadvantages, compared to more traditional fundraising methods—a comparison that will help you understand why affinity fundraising might be a preferred method for your organization.

To ensure success, it is of primary importance that the right volunteers be chosen for affinity fundraising. We'll show you how to identify individuals who have the skills, motivation, and attitude necessary for success.

But first, you may be wondering why volunteers should be involved in the first place. Isn't fundraising a task for a professional development staff?

Why Involve Volunteers in Fundraising?

Volunteers Give More

Volunteerism is a key factor in charitable giving. Surveys indicate that (1) households with a volunteer give nearly twice the percentage of household income as contributing households in which the respondent does not volunteer, and (2) during an economic recession, giving does not decline as long as volunteerism does not decline.[1]

> Nonprofit organizations have a limited budget with which to hire staff. Think for a moment how much more you could accomplish with volunteers:
>
> - How many more prospects could be visited
> - How many more people would hear about your important work in the community
> - How many more could contribute
> - How many more donors would develop a deeper understanding of how important your mission really is

Involve volunteers and you will multiply your results.

The shortest distance to the donor is through the volunteer.

Volunteers Have More Influence Than Staff

Volunteers can communicate more effectively with prospective donors than staff can. Volunteers work for different reasons from staff; fundraising isn't simply part of their job description. They donate their own time and resources because they believe deeply in the organization. Their conviction and altruism is the candle that ignites the fire.

Volunteers Attract Others Who Are Committed

What you will discover is that greater volunteer involvement will fuel the growth of a larger, more committed pool of donors and organizational stakeholders. By nurturing the interests of your special volunteers, you will be able to secure the support and resources necessary to achieve the goals of your organization.

Who Has Potential for Affinity Fundraising?

Unfortunately, most nonprofit organizations involve volunteers primarily in the programmatic functions of the organization and have little or no experience with volunteers in fundraising efforts. This book will show you how to recruit and train select volunteers who have the required aptitude and skills.

We will not be concerned with volunteers whose involvement is sporadic or occasional. Our purposes are best served by concentrating on the individuals whose involvement is characterized by longevity and regularity, as well as those who have an emotional or personal involvement with the organization's mission. They have high affinity for the organization. These individuals are likely to participate in activities that are integral to the well-being of the organization. They might be board members, committee chairs, or key professional staff, including staff whose job description does not include fundraising activities. We will refer to this select group as the *core volunteers* (see Figure 1.1).

Characteristics of Core Volunteers

You can identify potential core volunteers because they

- Love the organization and care deeply about its future
- Have several years involvement as a donor, volunteer, or staff member
- May have already involved their families and friends in the organization
- Contribute their time or financial resources freely

Characteristics of Staff Members Who Become Core Volunteers

You can identify potential staff core volunteers because

- They often volunteer their personal time for special projects.
- The organization is their chief charitable involvement.
- Their morale is good; they feel adequately compensated and appreciated.

FIGURE 1.1

Core Volunteers and the Total Volunteer Population

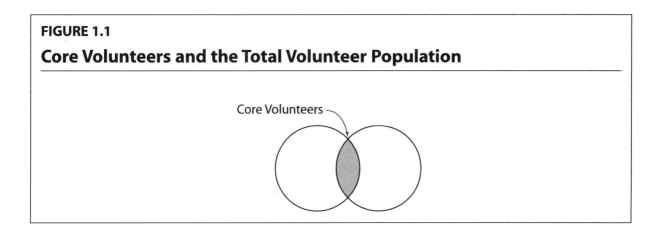

Core Volunteers

Why Do Some Volunteers and Staff Become Core Volunteers?

Some 80 percent of core volunteers actually are the best prospects for giving. Thus volunteers often become prospects and eventual donors (see Figure 1.2).

The reverse situation also occurs. A donor may wish to become a member of the core volunteer group because he or she realizes the opportunity and potential of surfacing significant gifts from others. The donor may wish to visit with other prospects. Also, individuals might move into or from various groups (see Figure 1.3).

Core volunteers provide the human resources required for affinity fundraising. They identify, prioritize, and visit with prospective donors (prospects). Because affinity fundraising is volunteer-driven, the volunteers eventually become involved in shaping and implementing the plan for capital, annual, endowment, planned, and special project giving.

FIGURE 1.2

Prospects Among Core Volunteers

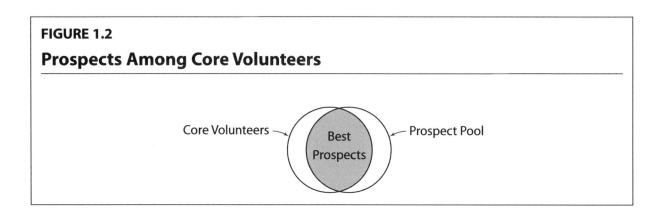

FIGURE 1.3

Possible Progressions of Individuals into Groups

Staff ⟶ core volunteer ⟶ prospect ⟶ donor

Donor ⟶ core volunteer

Core volunteer ⟶ prospect ⟶ donor

Prospect ⟶ donor ⟶ core volunteer

Prospect ⟶ core volunteer ⟶ donor

Perhaps you question whether your organization has potential core volunteers or whether you have enough core volunteers to make a difference. In Chapter Four we will help you identify your core volunteers. Subsequent chapters will help you expand that group into a committed group of leaders. You will also learn how to cultivate individuals to higher levels of affinity. But whether you have one or one hundred core volunteers, you can start building your affinity fundraising program today.

Two Approaches to Fundraising: Traditional and Affinity

Here is a way to compare affinity fundraising with the traditional approach:

In the traditional approach to fundraising: identify those with the greatest wealth (who may or may not have connections with the organization); ask directly for contributions.

In affinity fundraising: identify individuals closest to the organization; listen and respond to their most important interests, values, and beliefs; invite their participation in areas that interest them and that validate their personal needs.

Let us discuss the advantages and disadvantages of both approaches.

The Traditional Approach

Many fundraising professionals, ourselves included, have used the traditional direct approach, which involves targeting wealthy people or their friends. When volunteers are involved, they may be asked to target those friends or colleagues and convert them to the nonprofit's agenda. The scenario in which "one hand washes the other" does work well with the affluent. However, the inherent difficulty of this approach is that it falters when used with the general, charitable population. Many individuals may be resistant to or offended by the conversion process. Moreover, many prospective donors have their own priorities regarding charitable giving. It is difficult to convert individuals who have little or no affinity for the nonprofit's work.

For all these reasons, the traditional approach may be discouraging for volunteers who are faced with a dual job: (1) to educate or sell the prospect on the organization and its mission and (2) to ask for a gift. The end result is that volunteers may feel overwhelmed and not complete their calls. In the long term, professionals often need to do the mop-up work, which overburdens a campaign that may already be understaffed.

Staff members, because of their expertise or knowledge, are usually more likely to complete personal calls. However, many organizations lack the staffing required to solicit the number of prospects necessary to complete a campaign. Another consideration may be staff's lack of experience with personal solicitation. For most nonprofit managers, the face-to-face visit is not a large part of their everyday agenda. Consequently, many development personnel are reluctant to make personal calls.

Another shortcoming with the direct approach is that it limits the number of prospects. Overuse of wealth indicators as a priority factor shortchanges the organization. This method overlooks vast numbers of potential donors. It overlooks a significant number of individuals who may not be considered wealthy by traditional attributes of affluence but who are nonetheless capable of making significant gifts. Moreover, it overlooks the potential of volunteers, who often become your best contributors.

Traditional fundraising campaigns focus on an individual's cash flow, or net income, which limits the possibility of securing a prospect's greatest source of charitable dollars—total net worth. This is a much larger pot of potential dollars that includes an individual's total lifetime accumulations. It may include insurance, stocks, bonds, and real estate, as well as current or expected income from individuals and businesses. Affinity fundraising creates opportunities for donors to donate from this larger pot of money, based on their individual needs and interests (see Figure 1.4).

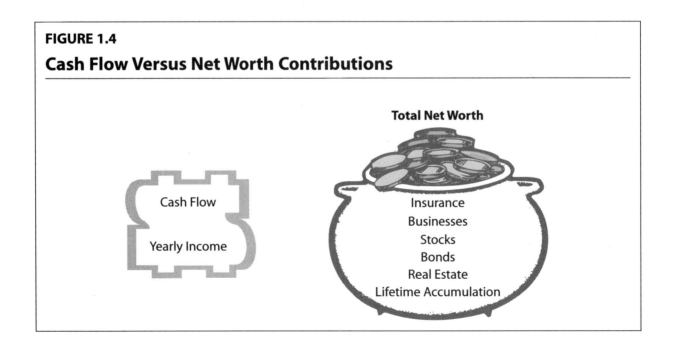

FIGURE 1.4

Cash Flow Versus Net Worth Contributions

Cash Flow

Yearly Income

Total Net Worth

Insurance
Businesses
Stocks
Bonds
Real Estate
Lifetime Accumulation

Contrast the situation just described with the more traditional method in which donors typically move *up* the pyramid, increasing gift size. Usually donors are not solicited for estate gifts unless they have demonstrated a long history of giving or significant charitable involvement. The comparison of affinity and traditional fundraising is shown in Figure 1.5.

The Affinity Fundraising Approach

In affinity fundraising it is the volunteer's first task to ascertain a prospect's willingness to make estate gifts. Once the prospect makes this important decision, the person can be solicited for other types of giving, as appropriate. In the affinity model, donors typically move *up and down* the pyramid, participating in multiple giving opportunities.

One presumed advantage of the traditional fundraising method is that it is considered a faster method of securing funds. In some cases this is true. It is usually quicker and easier to get smaller gifts. Although in some cases affinity fundraising might require more time, we believe that in the long term, affinity fundraising will secure greater resources for the organization.

Affinity fundraising fits naturally with volunteer leadership. Because volunteers are asked only to visit with individuals who have an affinity for the nonprofit, the job becomes less threatening, less like fundraising, and more like fun. This process minimizes the fear that many volunteer solicitors experience due to lack of experience or to unpleasant fundraising experiences.

With affinity fundraising, the emphasis is not on the "ask" but on listening and building relationships. You will notice this distinction as you

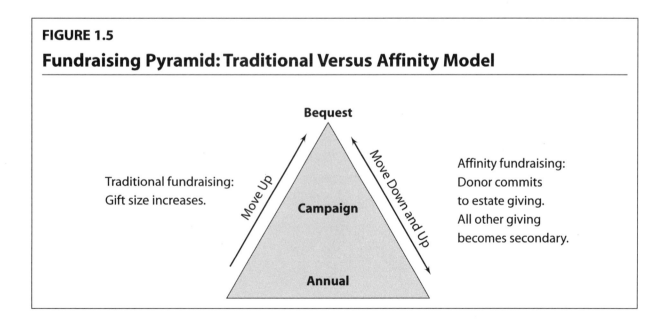

FIGURE 1.5

Fundraising Pyramid: Traditional Versus Affinity Model

Bequest

Move Up

Move Down and Up

Traditional fundraising: Gift size increases.

Campaign

Affinity fundraising: Donor commits to estate giving. All other giving becomes secondary.

Annual

proceed through the following chapters. Volunteers are not trained in fundraising. Fundraising terminology is never used. The phrase "fundraising training" could intimidate volunteers because their prior experiences may have demonstrated that fundraising is an undesirable activity. Instead, volunteers receive "coaching in making personal visits."

Volunteers will be guided through the process, step by step. They will learn only what they need to know in order to successfully complete each step. Because this process is less overwhelming, volunteers tend to complete their assignments and normally don't experience the burnout that volunteers experience when they use the direct approach. Experience shows that approximately 80 percent of volunteers who participate in affinity fundraising training meetings complete their calls.

Rather than confine prospects to cash contributions, affinity fundraising opens the door to transfer-of-wealth resources. The scripting techniques of affinity fundraising, learned through practice role plays of the interview format, identify individuals who are predisposed to estate-type giving. Our experience indicates that after individuals make a commitment to planned giving, all other types of giving become inconsequential by comparison. Moreover, in addition to estate-type giving, the donor's goals, values, interests, and cash flow resources can more easily be aligned to benefit annual, campaign, or special project objectives.

Note

1. *Giving and Volunteering in the U.S.: Findings from Six National Surveys.* INDEPENDENT SECTOR, 1999.

Chapter 2

Assessing Your Organization's Level of Affinity

WHICH PEOPLE are most likely to help your organization? When asked this question, most nonprofit staff members consider only those of wealth and influence in the community. Yet these individuals may not be the best prospects. Many times they are being solicited by multiple organizations for causes that present little or no affinity for their personal needs, interests, and goals. In this chapter you will learn how to find the often-overlooked philanthropists who *are* likely to help your organization.

Equally important is that you will learn how to complete the affinity chart, or grid—a tool to help you estimate your organization's potential for success with affinity fundraising. Based on donor, stakeholder, and organization characteristics, the affinity chart will help you determine whether your organization tends toward *high affinity* or *low affinity.* High-affinity organizations may be able to surface large gifts in sixty to ninety days, whereas low-affinity organizations may need to spend time cultivating their existing high-affinity core volunteers into a committed group of leaders and raising overall levels of affinity for the organization.

Questions and answers that appear at the end of the chapter will help you characterize your organization further as *more* low affinity or high affinity. High-affinity nonprofits are already over-positioned for fundraising success. There is no need for them to spend time and money to get ready.

How to Find Untapped Philanthropists

When searching for major gift prospects, many nonprofit managers look to those of obvious wealth in the surrounding community. Undeniably, ability to give is a major factor in fundraising. Yet how does one discover those with an ability to give? Many potential donors do not live a wealthy lifestyle. By traditional standards these individuals might not be considered wealthy, but they are still good prospects. And they are within the reach of every nonprofit organization.

Later in this chapter you will learn how affinity fundraising can help you uncover these often-overlooked philanthropists. Cultivate them and you will discover a treasure chest of human and financial resources.

Consider the following example, which illustrates that donors who make significant gifts may not necessarily live a wealthy lifestyle.

CASE EXAMPLE: MILDRED AND BILL PETERS

After graduation from the University of Minnesota College of Pharmacy, Bill Peters operated a small drug store in Minneapolis. By outward appearances, the Peters did not have a wealthy lifestyle; their home was a modest, one-bedroom apartment. One of their few extravagances was owning a late-model Cadillac. When asked what motivated him to give, Bill stated that he attributed every success in his life to what he had learned at the university.

During their lifetimes, the Peters donated nearly $3 million to pharmacy-related projects at the University of Minnesota. Childless and without close relatives, the Peters gave $14 million of their estate to the College of Pharmacy.

How Dollars Follow Values

The concept that dollars follow values is central to affinity fundraising. Donors give in direct relationship to their values, attitudes, and beliefs. Affinity fundraising will help you discover and learn the importance of these attributes.

The interview form shown in Chapter Five (Worksheet 5.2, "Sample Interview Script") provides open-ended questions that help identify a prospect's core values, attitudes, and beliefs. You will learn how to ask these pertinent questions in a conversational manner, as well as how to interpret and organize the responses. You will learn how to develop a specific prospect cultivation plan that responds to the unique needs of each individual.

For example, read the following statements. What important values do they convey?

"I think children should have an early opportunity to succeed in school." (Value: We must reach children early to equip them for a successful life.)

"Many elderly people need to find a way to avoid loneliness or isolation." (Value: Socialization is important for the elderly so they can avoid loneliness.)

An "Organizational Affinity Chart" appears in Worksheet 2.1. You may wish to make a copy of this chart and indicate by making a check mark whether the descriptions fit your organization. If you feel that your organization has more of the characteristics on the left side of the chart, then your organization has higher levels of affinity. Similarly, you may feel that some of your organizational characteristics are more appropriately described on the low-affinity side of the chart.

You may discover that you have higher levels of affinity in some areas than others. For example, under "number of prospects" you may have many (fifty or more) volunteers who contribute financially. At the same time, however, you may have a poor history of financial management, which is a low-affinity characteristic.

Organizations that experience the greatest success are typically those whose characteristics tend to cluster on the high-affinity side of the chart. These organizations have the fewest barriers to involvement. They have many who care, financial management is not an issue, and their programs or services are well respected and needed.

Questions You May Ask

I work for a small organization that was just started. Does this mean that we are low affinity?

Not necessarily. Size or longevity is not necessarily correlated to affinity levels. If your mission is an attraction to many individuals, this works in your favor. Also, if your programs or services have a good track record and reputation, this further enhances your affinity characteristics.

Small organizations may have a small group of core volunteers to start, but if they have high-affinity characteristics, they will be able to expand this group rather quickly. This will be explained more fully in subsequent chapters.

According to the affinity chart (Worksheet 2.1), our organization's characteristics seem to be clustered under low affinity. We just formed our organization and have few donors. Does that mean that we should not do affinity fundraising?

Absolutely not! If you are a small organization with little track record or a mission that is narrow in focus or perhaps politically unfavorable, you will experience greater challenges. Still, even low-affinity organizations can achieve results.

WORKSHEET 2.1

Organizational Affinity Chart

High Affinity		Low Affinity

High Affinity

Maturity in service
- Programs are highly valued.
- Organization is recognized for excellence.
- Many benefit from services or programs.

Type of mission
- Mission of organization provides a solution.

Image of stability
- Record of fiscal management is solid.
- Community leaders and key representatives support the organization.
- History of community benefit is long.

Longevity of staff, donors, and volunteers
- Volunteers have many years of involvement.
- Donors have many years of support.
- Staff retention levels are high.

Levels of ownership
- Volunteers care about the cause.
- Donors involve families and friends.
- Volunteers involve families and friends.
- Staff indicates a willingness to volunteer for special projects.
- Volunteers want to do more.

Leadership
- Board, managers, and leaders are committed to development.

Number of prospects
- Large numbers of volunteers make financial contributions.
- Large numbers of staff make financial contributions.

Low Affinity

- Programs are new or of unknown value.
- Track record is marginal or nonexistent.
- Few benefit.

- Mission is weak, controversial, or duplicative of others' efforts.

- History of fiscal management is poor or nonexistent.
- Community or key leaders give little support.

- History of community benefit is short.

- Volunteers are newly involved or have little history of involvement.
- Few donors are involved; most are recent contributors.
- Staff retention levels are low.

- Volunteers work for personal reasons.
- Donors have not involved others in the organization.
- Volunteers have not involved others in the organization.
- Staff is reluctant to participate beyond necessity.
- Volunteers are marginally interested in expanding the organization.

- Leaders are skeptical or avoid participation in development.

- Few volunteers contribute.
- Few or no staff contribute financially.

Consider the Whitman Foundation, the arm of an inner-city, public elementary school. Although the school had no annual fund and no fundraising experience other than receiving a grant or two each year, the new board was able to raise $30,000 in its first year. How? In their founding year, they developed a twelve-member board of directors. More than 60 percent of the school families were of low income. Similarly, board members were not wealthy according to traditional measures of affluence. Still, the board members, who were teachers, parents, and alumni, did possess the important characteristics of high affinity. Working together, they were determined to raise funds for school programs and services.

Their first activity was to host an informal party where the goals of the foundation would be highlighted. All invitees were high-affinity individuals: those who were identified by board members and staff as those who cared most about the school and its students. After this party, individual friends and board members were solicited and $30,000 was secured within six months. Today the foundation continues to expand its activities and expects to more deeply involve alumni, parents, teachers, and other high-affinity individuals.

We are a religious community with no fundraising staff. Could affinity fundraising be of benefit?

Yes. Faith communities often do not have fundraising staff, and yet many have the characteristics of high-affinity organizations. Why? Because faith communities have large groups of followers who believe deeply in the mission of the organization. Although many of these individuals have not been cultivated by professional fundraisers, many will be willing to contribute significantly and become involved as a core volunteer to ensure the future of the religious community.

Is it possible to secure immediate gifts?

Yes, it is possible for some organizations to surface gifts in a matter of months. Although it is of primary importance to match the donor's time schedule, you will also learn how to encourage prospects to donate their money today rather than tomorrow. The initial prospect visit sets the tone for this by asking specific questions that pertain to the prospect's willingness to give and his or her desire to help the nonprofit. As donors begin to realize that they have more than enough income for their present and future needs, they begin to funnel the surplus resources to their beloved charity.

How to Combat Skepticism

It is natural and healthy for you to experience a certain degree of skepticism about affinity fundraising. Why is this so? Generous donors have been misled and manipulated often enough to have reason for legitimate skepticism. Therefore, legitimate skepticism is a natural part of the introduction to a new, nonmanipulative fundraising experience. Once affinity fundraising is experienced, this skepticism will dissolve.

The affinity fundraising model is a strong and stable source of revenues and human resources for all types of organizations. Start today to develop a listening project, using the steps outlined for affinity fundraising. As you progress, you will discover a treasure chest of human and financial resources.

Part Two

Getting the Organization Ready

Chapter 3

Reaping Results Through Staff and Volunteer Collaboration

THIS CHAPTER provides a framework to help you understand how to integrate human resources in affinity fundraising to accomplish your organization's development goals. Included is a discussion of leadership style, an overview of the steps necessary to implement the first phase of an affinity fundraising program, and a case example that describes how one organization involved staff and volunteers in continued planning and implementation beyond the initial Listening Project.

Leadership and Affinity Fundraising

As you implement the affinity fundraising model, you may experience a shift in your work style with individuals. Certain elements are required if you are to be successful.

• Relationships with the core volunteers of the organization must be developed.

• Organization leaders, the board chair, and the executive director must include the core volunteers in planning and decision making because a consensus style of leadership is most conducive to success. When fundraising plans are driven by core volunteers, they will be more likely to contribute their time and resources.

• Key staff members should become working partners with members of the core volunteer group. They must be prepared to work alongside volunteers in a primarily volunteer-driven effort. It is not essential that all staff be involved, but experience indicates that staff involvement significantly enhances results for many organizations. Your goal should be to develop the individuals who have both an interest and the appropriate skills to make personal visits. These individuals may be volunteers, staff, or a combination of both.

Four Steps to Completing Affinity Fundraising

Many organizations refer to the first phase (the initial four steps) of affinity fundraising as the Listening Project. This name appropriately describes one of the key behaviors that contributes to success. In the following chapters we will discuss in greater detail how to complete the steps we describe next.

Step 1: Estimate Fundraising Potential

In Chapter Two you learned how to assess whether your organization has high or low levels of affinity. Although all nonprofit organizations can begin immediately, organizations with high levels of affinity will have many potential core volunteers and correspondingly will have greater potential for surfacing human and financial resources.

Step 2: Identify Your Core Group

In the next chapter you will learn how to conduct a meeting of potential core volunteers. These individuals will help you determine who your best volunteers and prospects are. You will learn what behavioral characteristics, attitudes, and attributes describe the core volunteer as well as the best prospect. Working from the existing database of records, the development office will then supply a list of individuals who possess the required characteristics; the core volunteers will identify those individuals whom they feel have the highest affinity. These can then be priority ranked as the best prospects for subsequent personal visits.

Step 3: Prepare Volunteers for Listening Visits

At the orientation meeting described in Chapter Five, you will distribute an interview form (Worksheet 5.2) to the core volunteers. This form introduces a scripting technique that tells your core volunteers what to say when they interview the high-affinity individuals (prospects) whom their peers have identified. This script significantly increases the volunteers' comfort level because they know exactly what to say in order to achieve success. By the end of this meeting, your core volunteers will choose five individuals to interview.

Step 4: Evaluate and Report Listening Results

Excitement builds among core volunteers as they share the results of their personal visits in a group meeting. The responses to the open-ended questions in the interview form will indicate

- Which interviewees are good core volunteer candidates

- Which interviewees have no intention of giving (usually 10–20 percent)

- The priority ranking of individuals as to the strength of their affinity and their willingness to give

- Which individuals are likely to make estate gifts

- Which individuals are likely to become involved in campaigns or special projects

You will learn that the core volunteers are often willing to continue their efforts with prospective donors. The core volunteers realize the tremendous importance of their continued involvement in the Listening Project. They realize that they are the connecting bridge between the prospect and the nonprofit organization. They also realize that they are the necessary link to protect confidential information, as well as the ideal person to transfer the friend to someone who can help them complete their philanthropic agenda. They will begin to look at their own ability to make more significant charitable gifts to the organization.

Perhaps you might be saying to yourself, "Yes, but we are a small nonprofit. I'm not sure whether we have *any* core volunteers." Or you might say, "We are too new. No one knows about us." Try to block these thoughts. We will help you identify and cultivate certain core volunteers who, over time, will become your greatest contributors.

The following case example, which describes an organization in a small town in a rural area, shows how organizations without technical expertise and fundraising staff can successfully implement affinity fundraising. All names have been changed for purposes of confidentiality.

CASE EXAMPLE: PIONEER RETIREMENT COMMUNITY (PRC)

PRC is a seventy-year-old care center for the elderly; it plans to build a special care facility to meet the needs of people with Alzheimer's disease. Key points relative to the case are that the organization

- Has the characteristics of a high-affinity organization, with many potential core volunteers and prospects.
- Has no professional fundraiser on payroll. Although the organization's corporate board was highly motivated, the newly formed foundation board had never raised funds for the organization.
- Had no prior annual fund.

- Has an executive director who was convinced that without a permanent endowment fund, the home would cease to exist.
- Has leadership (board and executive) committed to the project.

Timeline and Planning
Phase 1
The initial Listening Project visits were completed in three months.

Within six months the organization raised $250,000.

Key leaders learned who would be the best leaders for each committee.

Phase 2
The leaders recruited these individuals for their respective committees:

- Annual Fund Program
- Alzheimer's Campaign
- Endowment, Bequests, or Big-Gifts Program
- Marketing and Communications

The leaders decided that the Listening Project would become the centerpiece of the overall development program. During this same year they planned to launch an endowment program.

Phase 3
The affinity fundraising program continues. Leaders are now using the Listening Project as an alternative to a traditional feasibility study in which interviews are conducted to determine whether sufficient prospects and volunteers are available for a capital campaign.

Figure 3.1 shows a project organizational chart that illustrates the workflow of staff and volunteers.

The Organization
The Chair
Bob, a highly respected chaplain, had been a leader in the local Alzheimer's community. As a former pastor, Bob had interviewed many of the best friends of PRC in the Listening Project; he knew many as former members of his religious community. A recent widower, Bob gave testimony in the report meeting about how his personal participation as a core volunteer had helped him in his own estate planning.

FIGURE 3.1

Sample Project Organizational Chart

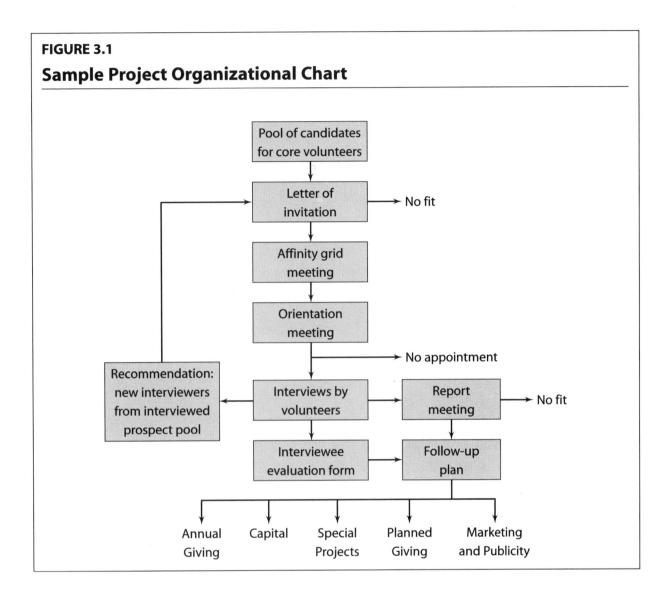

The Leadership

Leaders of the following committees were high-affinity volunteers with volunteer experience in the organization, but the majority had no prior fundraising experience with the organization.

Planned Giving

The interviews conducted during the Listening Project identified many potential bequest and planned giving candidates. Rene, a highly respected community volunteer, renamed this original core committee, the Listeners. "Where can you find someone to listen to you in today's world?" Rene wondered out loud. She personally recruited every one of the volunteers, who attended another training program beyond the initial phase of the Listening Project.

Staff Participation

Six staff members were involved: two housing directors, a volunteer director, a former chaplain, and two social workers.

Robert Daly, a donor who was interviewed by a staff social worker, was identified as an estate donor only as a result of the Listening Project. Shortly, in consultation with his attorney, he decided that he could afford to give $250,000 outright. Other potential estate donors were identified.

Campaign Donor Involvement

Core volunteers who participated in the Listening Project and who had a history of campaign leadership were identified as potential leaders for the next campaign. New candidates for campaign leadership with a long history of connections to the retirement community were also identified.

Marketing and Communications

Robert Daly, initially considered as an estate donor, decided that he could begin giving earlier; he created a $250,000 endowment fund. He now presents $250 checks as annual gift awards to every employee of the organization as a reward for their outstanding service. The gifts have been an excellent retention incentive for staff.

Robert hopes to inspire others with his efforts. Acknowledgment events have been ongoing, with luncheons for donors who have made significant one-time or cumulative gifts. Robert has and continues to share his own motivation for giving as a speaker at these events. The local newspaper has also published Robert's testimonials. Starting out as a prospect, Robert moved quickly to donor and then core volunteer. He now schedules listening interviews with others who have been identified as prospects.

Annual Fund

A board member was responsible for obtaining a $50,000, three-year-renewable matching grant. A significant match like this can always be used to jump-start the annual fund.

Remember that no matter the size, age, or shape of your organization, volunteers can help you secure major gifts. Additionally, it is useful to remember that although we have identified the four steps necessary to implement a Listening Project, every organization is different; you may need fewer or more steps to accomplish your goals.

Small organizations with low-affinity characteristics start the affinity fundraising model on a smaller scale. Key leaders may start by meeting with the organization's highest-affinity individuals in a series of individual meetings rather than meeting with groups of individuals. Similarly, you may wish to meet with individuals informally rather than in highly structured group sessions. Your small number of individuals will grow from one to five and more as time progresses. Additional ideas for building affinity will be explored further in Chapter Nine. Gradually you will develop a group of committed leaders.

Upon completion of these initial steps, core volunteers are usually ready to plan and implement a more extensive affinity fundraising model that includes an endowment, capital or project campaign, or annual giving fund. Each organization develops its committees according to its unique needs, as determined by the core volunteers. As you progress through subsequent chapters, you will learn in greater detail how to complete Steps 1–4 of the Listening Project—the first phase of affinity fundraising.

Chapter 4

Identifying High-Affinity Prospects and Volunteers

THIS CHAPTER describes how you can complete Step 2 of the Listening Project. You will learn how to encourage high-affinity individuals to use the affinity grid—a tool for charting the behavioral and personal characteristics of individuals who care about the organization. Those identified will become your best prospects for subsequent personal visits.

Four actions are required for successful completion of the affinity grid meeting:

1. Identify the characteristics of high-affinity individuals.
2. Identify individuals who possess these characteristics.
3. Prioritize the list, ranking the most frequently identified individuals as the highest priority.
4. Identify a smaller subset of individuals as the individuals who have the attributes necessary to be volunteers.

Preparations for the Affinity Grid Meeting

Who Should Be Invited?

The ideal mix is to have more volunteers than staff. If the reverse is true, a volunteer-driven environment will not predominate. The group should be small, with no more than eighteen to twenty volunteers attending. As a rule, larger organizations tend to invite up to twenty individuals, whereas smaller organizations may invite only five.

The invitees are people who have an extensive history with the organization and who care deeply about the mission of the organization. They will be able to answer the following question: "In your opinion, who cares more about the mission of the organization than anyone else you can think of?"

The potential invitees may be

- Long-term staff or retired staff who know senior constituents and their families

- Volunteers who have wide and varied experience and therefore knowledge of who has been involved in the history of the organization

- Bequest donors and long-term donors (not always essential, as affinity fundraising is also applicable to younger, high-affinity individuals)

If you have a large number of attendees who are in retirement or are approaching retirement, this is positive. Although people in their thirties and forties may think about estate planning, older people have most likely begun to think more specifically about how to distribute their financial resources. The exceptions to this rule are individuals who have acquired substantial wealth in their earlier years and are philanthropically inclined. Entrepreneurs and technology developers might be members of the latter group. Serious health problems are also an exception.

Because your invitees have a history with the organization, they will be able to identify people who care most about it. They may know those people personally and may have observed their work with the organization. Thus they can identify them from a refined list that will be prepared by the development staff.

Who Should Not Be Invited?

This is not a traditional campaign prospect selection meeting, where people with multigenerational, inherited wealth and perceived community movers and shakers would be prime invitees.

Neither should you invite single-issue individuals who would have difficulty working cooperatively with others in a consensus-driven agenda. They may be less likely to listen to the opinions of others. If you have high-affinity friends with these characteristics, invite them to participate at a later time, in a role that best suits their interests, experience, and temperament.

Preparation for the Meeting

First, prepare the newsprint sheets. Using the affinity grid (see Table 4.1), prepare one newsprint sheet that replicates these headings: Linkage, Interest, Signals, Values, Age, and Ability. By the end of the meeting, your participants will have given you information to fill several sheets. These are to be placed on the wall around the room.

TABLE 4.1

Affinity Grid: Characteristics of High-Affinity Individuals

Linkage	Interest	Signals	Values	Age	Ability

Second, consider how you will set the tone of the meeting. It should convey a feeling of personal closeness, caring, and support.

Next consider the goal of the meeting: to identify the individuals who have the greatest affinity, that is, devotion and ownership for the mission of the nonprofit. You read in Chapter One some ways to differentiate core volunteers from everyday volunteers. Every organization has candidates for the core volunteer group. You can find them among your current volunteers and donors, current and past staff, and past founders. They will exhibit the following characteristics and behaviors:

- The mission of your organization is often one of their top priorities.

- They rarely miss a meeting or event.

- They are eager to participate and help.

- They contribute time and dollars to one or more areas within the organization (size of gift is not necessarily important).

- They may have a special interest within the organization for which they contribute much volunteer time or financial support.

The objectives for the affinity grid meeting are to

- Create the first draft of the affinity grid

- Identify no more than one hundred prospects to interview (those with the highest affinity or priority)

- Identify and recruit core volunteers

- Build and increase the volunteers' sense of ownership by expecting their participation in the next meeting—the orientation meeting

- Establish the criteria that staff will use to compile (the same day or within twenty-four hours) an extensive list of volunteers and prospects

Important tasks before the meeting are:

- Schedule the day and time of the meeting to meet the needs of the attendees, not the organization.

- Mail the letter of invitation, which is found at the end of this chapter, to confirm the date and give a crisp description of the purpose for the meeting.

- Place a follow-up call to confirm attendance within forty-eight hours after the letter is received.

- Place reminder calls the day before the meeting.

The seating and table arrangement should allow all participants to see each other. Wall space should be available on which to post large sheets of newsprint for notes.

Supplies for the meeting should include

- Colored markers and pencils

- Name tags and name tents

- Newsprint easel paper, with sticky back, so that sheets can be placed around the room (six to eight sheets to be placed within an hour)

- Newsprint sheets

Make the newsprint sheets in advance, replicating the affinity grid headings. These sheets will be used to describe characteristics of high-affinity people. Allow plenty of room under each heading to write comments that demonstrate the criteria.

Refined List of Prospects

The development office is responsible for preparing a *quality prospect list*, which should be alphabetized and contain fewer than five hundred names. The list should be short enough that the participants can peruse the names in less than twenty minutes; they will then select individuals from the list whom they believe have the highest affinity.

Those to be included on the refined prospect list should be

- People who always attend special events or programs

- Donors who have the longest history of giving

- Board members (present and former)

- Retirees or their survivors

- Volunteers and officers with a long history

- Individuals whose family and friends have participated for many years

- Those recognized as leaders within the charity's community of stakeholders

Lists should be alphabetized by name; the city should be included but nothing else. Large type and double-spacing should be used if possible.

It is important to be age-sensitive. If the list gets too long, focus on those who are sixty and older. If the computer doesn't track age, the list must be culled to remove younger prospects. In some cases, young, successful entrepreneurs may be candidates, but most people don't begin their estate planning until later in life. As we mentioned earlier, it is important to concentrate on individuals who are in the "distribution phase" of life—a time when they are considering how to distribute their resources.

How to Conduct the Meeting

First, the chairperson or a designate asks everyone to introduce themselves. Request that they limit their comments to their names and a brief history of their involvement to one minute.

Distribute the Agenda

Tell participants that they will take part in an exercise that identifies the organization's top ten to one hundred friends. Describe the friends as those who have high affinity or high ownership in the ongoing mission of the organization.

Remind participants that they will identify individuals without mentioning names or breaking any confidences. Indeed, many will already be sitting in the room. In close communities others may recognize or have a good idea whom you are describing. Why? They are thinking of the same individual!

Allow only one person to participate at a time. Determine in advance who are the more verbal attendees. Let those who have a reputation for being expressive go first; however, remember that quieter participants also make powerful comments.

Discuss the Affinity Grid

Note that you will ask participants to describe the personal characteristics or behaviors that describe an individual who cares about the organization. This exercise will eventually enable the group to identify the specific individuals who possess the characteristics of high affinity. The entire exercise is confidential and names are never mentioned.

The leader might say: "I'd like you (the assembled group) to think of the person who, in your opinion, has the greatest love, appreciation, feeling, involvement, and devotion for our organization. Please do not think of these individuals in terms of whether they have, would, or should make a gift. We don't need to know that. What we need to know is who appreciates and loves the organization."

Sometimes a participant will answer, "I can think of several people." Respond as follows: "That's great, but could we think of one friend at a time? Describe the connections your first person has had with our organization. Who would like to go first?" Ask the most verbal participants to answer these questions if there is a lull in participation:

How would you describe the person? Please use descriptive adjectives.

Why did that person come to mind?

What has he or she done for the organization?

What activities has he or she participated in?

Record the information on the newsprint sheets. While the initial responses are in process, uncover the easel sheet containing the outline of the affinity grid. Under each heading, write the descriptive phrases in the appropriate places on the sheet.

You might ask about the age of the party under discussion early in the exercise. Remember that not only are older people usually closer to making decisions about the distribution of their financial resources, they are usually more attuned to values, priority, and mortality.

Frequently, values intensify with advancing age because

• Years often bring a greater concern for the world.

• Years bring a greater concern for the next generation.

• Individuals often have a good idea as to what they want to do for their heirs.

• Older individuals have often assessed their priorities.

Another question is whether the person being discussed is considered wealthy. Discuss the "ability" qualifier in detail. It is not necessary to consider an individual's net worth. Nonetheless, we do not want to waste time and resources visiting an appreciative friend who receives public assistance.

Continue to ask others to participate in the same manner and continue to fill in the newsprint sheets. Try to continue generating behaviors and characteristics of high-affinity people until the group has exhausted their thinking on the topic.

You may wish to schedule a break or lunch period at this point. After the break, ask those present to share what has motivated them to be so connected for so many years. The recorder for the affinity grid then adds these comments to the sheets.

Distribute and Discuss the List (fifteen to twenty minutes)

Ask participants to peruse the list and identify individuals who display the high-affinity characteristics mentioned earlier in the meeting. Each participant will view their own list and place a check mark next to the names of individuals who possess these characteristics.

Two reminders are important here. First, sometimes people are listed who have been described only once on the grid. This is a mistake. Think only of friends who are described repeatedly (five to ten times) under the multiple criteria. Second, participants should think about the high-affinity friends of the nonprofit rather than their own personal friends.

Distribute Criteria for the Ideal Volunteer

Ask participants to review their list of names once again. Considering only the names that have already been checked, place a "V" (for volunteer) beside the names of the friends who fit these criteria (see Exhibit 4.1).

If the right people have been invited to this meeting, the nonprofit may not need a large number of additional volunteers. Many of today's participants will want to attend the orientation meeting to follow. Lower-affinity organizations may wish to work with their existing group and continue to expand to a larger group of committed leaders.

Distribute the Staff-Volunteer Recruitment Letter

Read the recruitment letter (see Exhibit 4.2) to all present; many will agree to attend the orientation meeting. Note that the meeting date has already been scheduled.

CASE EXAMPLE: HIGH-AFFINITY CHARACTERISTICS

It came as a total surprise from Dick Thompson, a quiet, unassuming, bachelor, jazz musician who, his friends said, "lived like he didn't have a dime." His habits were, to all appearances, modest in nature. For many years, Dick put $6 per week in the offering plate, never missing a week. If he happened to miss church, he personally dropped off his envelope at the church office on the following Monday. At one point, when the church was experiencing financial difficulty, he privately told a church worker to let him know if the church couldn't pay salaries or keep the lights on. "I know this is a tough time for the church, but things are going to be all right," he said. Dick surprised everyone when he left the church $2.5 million.

How would Dick have fit into an affinity meeting grid? Modest weekly giving over decades would have identified him under the heading, Linkage.

A long-term volunteer, he began his volunteer career at the church in the late 1970s, playing for services and various jazz

EXHIBIT 4.1

Criteria for the Ideal Volunteer

- Has long-term relationship with organization

- Received or observed life-changing benefits

- Is an attentive listener rather than a teller

- Enjoys personal interaction

- Is empathetic and caring

- Has the capacity to express feelings rather than protect privacy

- Has experienced personal misfortune

- Is respected by peers

- Keeps a confidence

- Is patient, not impatient

- Is broad-minded, not opinionated

- Is confident, not egocentric

- Avoids those who need to control others

- Is a retired employee

- Is approaching retirement age or is older

Note: *Self-employed people, teachers, nurses, social workers, people in the servicing professions, homemakers, engineers, clergy, analyticals, and managers have a history of good performance in conducting interviews.*

EXHIBIT 4.2

Staff-Volunteer Recruitment Letter

[Date]

Dear _____:

When we need help it is important to have friends we can go to for assistance. By all definitions you are a special friend of the Memorial Library.

This is an exciting time for the Memorial Library. The Archives and Access Center is soon to be completed, and donations are at an all-time record high.

To build on this momentum, I am pleased to invite you to a very important meeting, to be held on August 20th. A duplicate meeting will be held on September 1st. Both will run from 8–11 A.M.

The purpose of the meeting is to identify the criteria that will describe those friends who have the strongest feelings, loyalty, appreciation, and affection for the mission of Memorial Library. Your rich knowledge of and experience with the library over many years uniquely qualifies you to help us accomplish this objective.

I have asked _____*, our director of development, to call you within the next few days to confirm your availability and presence. If you prefer, feel free to call Judy at _____ .

Sincerely,

_____

Note: *The letter should be signed by someone the reader will recognize. This may be a volunteer or a staff person.*

concerts (another Linkage identifier). The quiet offer to help with payroll difficulties would have identified him under Signals messages during our affinity meeting. Dick's personal delivery of the envelope was another major Signal.

Here's a summary of the results of the prospect identification:

Prioritize your list of volunteers and prospects (see Figure 4.1 for an example). Assign a staff member to collate the prospect lists that have been checked off for prospects and volunteers. You will find that a small number of individuals have been identified repeatedly by more than one participant. These are your best prospects. If you are a low-affinity organization, start out with those who have been identified. Complete the Priority Prospect Chart the next day and send a copy to each of the meeting participants, attached to a thank-you (Exhibit 4.3). Note that no names appear, only the total number of prospects identified.

You may wish to make a chart for your organization, similar to the one that appears in Figure 4.1. Who are the special friends? Perhaps you have identified only three to five friends who can be characterized as high affinity. These individuals will be your best giving prospects.

Follow up promptly with volunteers. The day following the affinity grid meeting, send a thank-you memo to participants with a summary report of what they accomplished at the meeting.

Each organization will have a different configuration for the affinity grid. Review the following example of what the grid might look like for a library (Table 4.2). It may seem like an overly long list of characteristics. Keep in mind that the longer the list, the more identifiers are available to

---

FIGURE 4.1

Priority Prospect Chart

Number of core volunteers participating	Number of prospects identified	Cumulative Total	
21 or more	17	17	(Best prospects)
18–20	9	26	
15–17	24	50	
10–14	36	86	
5–9	71	157	

work with in identifying potential prospects and volunteers. A long list also shows that individuals possessing multiple affinity characteristics are likely to be better prospects.

Whether you have identified one or one hundred friends, the following chapters will meet your unique needs. We will provide you with step-by-step guidelines in how to develop your affinity fundraising program. Through a series of personal visits, you will learn the depth of the interviewees' relationship to your organization, as well as their intent to support your cause.

EXHIBIT 4.3

Thank-You Memo

DATE:
TO: [Take name from list of volunteers and staff present.]
FROM:

Ensuring a sound financial future through the Organization Endowment Program is within reach. That's why your presence on Tuesday, August 25th was so important. Our objective of using a small, select team to establish the criteria to describe [name of your organization]'s very best friends was achieved.

Your active participation and willingness to share your knowledge of the community enabled us to build a tailor-made "Affinity Grid" for the organization. We have enclosed a copy of this grid for your information. In addition, you enabled the foundation to clearly identify and rank [insert number] of our closest friends.

With appreciation for all you have done and are doing to continue [organization name]'s vital mission of serving present and future individuals.

Enclosure: Copy of the affinity grid

TABLE 4.2

Sample Affinity Grid for a Library

Linkage	Interest	Signals	Values	Age	Ability
Attendee of book club events	Attends all library events	Contributes to "Keeping the Memory Green"	Values	Older than fifty-five	Exclude only if demented or on public assistance
Collector	Asks for new events to be sponsored by library	Children; no interest in his interest	Work ethic	Retired or early retiree	Important only if multiple criteria are present
Founder	Comes to library every day; likes mission of libraries; sets tone for leadership	Widower without children	Frugal lifestyle	Very old	Friends often have discretionary income and net worth
Esteems work of the library		Donated personal collection	Spiritual values indicate support to others	Mature	
Librarian—retired; knowledgeable about collections	Family known for philanthropy, especially for libraries and education	Recruits others	Believes in library support of education	Young, if high-affinity friends with new wealth	Humble roots
Forty- to fifty-year history	Former head of government agency	Owns own business	Social service background		Inherited farms or funds
Multiyear donor, librarian		Simply loves books	Life-long learner		Spends nothing on self
Interested in literature	Library is where he wants to be	Collector, house full of books	Highbrow regarding classics		Executive or retired executive
Active in Friends of the Library		Anxious to visit	Education		Homeowner
Very active in collection	Loves books	Desires to help	Often conservative		
Rare collection	Loves reading	Very successful career	Wants to be part of other people's lives		
Member of advisory board	Prefers classics, information technology	Senior without family	Fosters life-long learning		
Close friend of primary donor		Retired executive	Service—the impact on people's lives—gives to future generations		
Ties to the collection	Works closely with researchers	Harshest critic			
Involved in lobbying	Fantastic collection	Repeat visitor			
Retired administrator	Worldwide contacts	Seeks opportunity			
Avocation has become passion	Knew curator as child	Initiates communications			
Constant user of collections	Has personal collection	No children or apparent heirs			
Participates in programs	Loves being around books and other people who love books	Devoted user			
Volunteers at library		Humanitarian			
Attends all professional meetings; never misses		Affinity for what we do, for the future			
Published by prestigious houses		Enthusiastic former staff			
Relationships with staff and volunteers		Initiates contacts			
Book or manuscript published		Curious			
Knew founder of collection		Extends above and beyond			
Grateful to library for going beyond call of duty		Avid reader			
		"My career would be nothing if it weren't for the library"			
		"Sensual—the touch and feel of a book"			
		"Library was the most important room in the house"			

Chapter 5

Helping Volunteers Conduct Donor Interviews

IF YOU have followed the steps outlined in the prior chapters, you have secured the volunteer support of your organization's most dedicated followers.

In this chapter we discuss how to train this committed group of core volunteers during the *orientation meeting*. There the volunteers will learn how to conduct a successful interview with their prospects. Here's an overview of the essentials of preparing for and conducting an orientation meeting:

- Send the Letter of Invitation to Interviewees (see Exhibit 5.1).

- Before the meeting, select an individual, either staff or volunteer, to participate in role plays during the meeting (see box on page 45).

- After the meeting starts, provide scripts and other instruction as needed.

- Distribute the worksheet, How to Get an Appointment for an Interview (see Worksheet 5.1).

- Conduct the role plays (see Exhibit 5.2, Handling Role Plays).

- Hold a feedback session following the role plays.

- Distribute the How to Estimate Net Worth form for use after the interviews, both role played and real (see Exhibit 5.3).

- Distribute the Interviewee Evaluation Form (see Worksheet 5.3) at the conclusion of each role play (to be used after the role plays and the real interviews).

- Schedule a *report meeting* to be held in four or five weeks after the orientation meeting to evaluate the interviews.

- Ask core volunteers to select five names of individuals to interview.

EXHIBIT 5.1

Letter of Invitation to Interviewees

[Name]
[Address]
[City, State, Zip]

Dear [name of prospect]:

We are thankful for our organization's long history of [appropriate text] to the people of [location]. Our loyal friends have played and will continue to play a significant role in our success.

The [organization name] is committed to continued excellence in our programs and services. To further our goals, we will be implementing a Pilot Research Project—a vital step toward ensuring that we will be able to serve present and future generations. This project will seek to learn how our closest supporters feel about our organization and to determine if there is any correlation between how our friends feel and the way they make decisions with respect to the distribution of their resources.

We plan to interview [number] of our closest friends before [date]. We hope that you will be able to participate so that we can learn your ideas and opinions and benefit from your life experience. You will not be solicited for funds.

Your candid reaction to this interview is absolutely essential for our planning. Within sixty days of the interview, you will receive a formal report, summarizing the findings and the collective, anonymous comments of all participants.

The following staff and volunteers will implement the project: [list of names].

I have personally endorsed this project because I am confident that your experience will be comfortable and instructive. One of our project members will telephone you within the next few days to schedule an appointment.

Sincerely,

[name of prominent sponsor]

WORKSHEET 5.1

How to Get an Appointment for an Interview

INTRODUCTION: Hello, this is _____ . I am calling about the Library's Pilot Research Project.

LETTER: Did you receive the letter from _____ , the university librarian, inviting you to participate?

SAY: This visit will take approximately 60 minutes. When would be the best time for us to visit? (Settle on a day first.)

DAY: Would [Monday] _____ A.M. or [Tuesday] _____ P.M. be better for you? (Settle on the time of day.)

TIME: Would 9:30 A.M. or 10:45 A.M. be better?

SAY: Good! I'll be looking forward to seeing you then.

PHONE: By the way, just in case some emergency comes up, I'd like to leave my telephone number. It is ( ) ___ - _____ . We can always reschedule.

If the prospect is reluctant to visit, try the following:

"Oh, I'm disappointed because we're only asking a select group to participate."

"Would you be willing to spend some time on _____ morning?"

EXHIBIT 5.2

Handling Role Plays

The role-play interview should take no longer than forty-five minutes. Simply read the questions and let the person being interviewed do 95 percent of the talking.

Tips for Role Players

- Don't play to the audience; look at each other.
- Maintain eye contact.
- The volunteer role player is more important than the form the interviewer uses.
- The volunteer should feel free to follow up with probing questions when a response is unclear.
- The interviewer should read the script exactly as written (no editorializing).

The interviewer completes a brief restatement and ends the visit. Everyone is ready for the feedback, which will take fifteen to thirty minutes. Ask the volunteers and staff present what was missed in the restatement. Lots, probably.

EXHIBIT 5.3

How to Estimate Net Worth

Key Question: How much might someone have to pass on to heirs?

You have listened to the interviewee and have observed firsthand:

- Family background
- Career path
- Living situation
- Lifestyle

Comparing your high-affinity prospect's situation with your own and that of your contemporaries, what would you guess is the value of his or her total estate?

Value	Number of Heirs	Amount
$100,000	1	$100,000
400,000	4	100,000
800,000	2	400,000
1,200,000	3	400,000
4,000,000	4	1,000,000

- Remind volunteer interviewers about the support system.
- Designate an individual, either staff or volunteer, to be the support person and to summarize the results of the interviews into report form.

> **How to Choose Volunteer Role Players**
>
> - Recruit volunteers in advance to participate in role-play exercises.
> - Ask two of the very responsive, newly recruited volunteers if they would be willing to participate in a role play.
> - Meet with the volunteers prior to the role-play exercises to increase their comfort level.
> - Spend about one hour on this exercise.
>
> *Note:* The professional staff should pay careful attention to how the volunteers react to the first role play. If a volunteer is applying the interview process to his or her own personal situation, it is quite apparent.

For further details about the meeting, you may wish to review the Sample Meeting Agenda (see Exhibit 5.4).

Tips on How to Succeed

In our work with volunteers and staff we have found that two factors contribute most to poor results with fundraising calls: (1) reluctance to call and (2) fear of failure. Our discussion will show how these pitfalls can be overcome so that maximum results can be achieved.

Another tip: *tell the core volunteers only what they need to know to take the next step.* That way they won't feel overwhelmed at first, and their excitement will build gradually.

Note that premature solicitation will short-circuit the true potential of your volunteers and your prospects. Volunteers should know up-front that they need not—in fact should not—ask for money during the first visit. The letter of invitation promises that. It also states that the topic of the interview will be the relationship between the prospect's feelings for the charity and the distribution of his or her financial resources.

Some high-affinity prospects may be convinced that the stated reason for the visit is just a ploy. But once they decide that the volunteer really *is* there to listen, they will open up and an intended forty-five-minute visit might last several hours.

These friends will offer their time and money when they are ready. The volunteer's role is not to talk people into parting with their money.

EXHIBIT 5.4

Sample Meeting Agenda

Agenda for Orientation Meeting
(approximately five hours)

Welcome and statement of vision

Introductions

Explanation of the foundation for success of the project:

- Encouragement that the affinity meeting provided

- Discussion of "present" and "desired" scenario

Presentation of role play #1

Feedback

Break

Presentation of role play #2

Feedback

Break

Distribution of support materials

Prospect selection

Lunch

Description of support system

Debriefing and questions

Adjournment

Even if a highly motivated interviewee offers a significant gift before the volunteer leaves, that gift should not be accepted on the spot. The volunteer should ask to hear more about this at a later time and arrange to see the person again.

Another possibility is prompt rejection, which is in fact cost-effective. This exercise is designed to help identify the friends who believe in your mission. Neither you nor your volunteers have time to convert people who have other agendas.

Who Should Be Invited to the Orientation Meeting?

Invite everyone who attended the affinity grid meeting or has otherwise expressed an interest in being a volunteer. You should also invite everyone who was identified at the affinity meeting as a potential volunteer for the project. As a rule of thumb, invite twice as many people as you need to complete the task.

Our experience indicates that individuals with multigenerational or inherited wealth rarely contribute their net worth. Their family tradition is to keep money within the family. These individuals will be identified as you learn to interpret the results of the interviews in Chapter Six; they should not be invited to these initial meetings. However, you will want to visit (interview) them. Depending on their responses, invite them to participate as a volunteer in a campaign or special project.

How to Prepare for the Orientation Meeting

Send the Letter of Invitation to Interviewees to the top prospects (seventy or fewer) who were chosen by staff and volunteers at the affinity grid meeting. Some organizations send fewer letters, depending on the number of prospects identified and the number of calls that volunteers can reasonably complete. Then choose a volunteer to participate in the interviewing role plays.

What to Expect from the Meeting

The outcomes of the orientation meeting should be to

- Remove all obstacles that cause failure
- Demonstrate that volunteers can surface money *without* the dreaded, direct "ask"

- Increase the comfort level of the volunteer interviewers through the practice of two role-play exercises

- Motivate the volunteer interviewers

- Teach the volunteers the characteristics of an ideal visit

- Secure the volunteers' commitment to complete three visits within three weeks

How to Conduct the Meeting

The leader opens the meeting with remarks similar to these:

We all have certain attitudes based on our experience. You've come here today willing to listen and possibly consider a volunteer [or professional staff] opportunity to interview some of our organization's best friends. You have been promised that you will not have to ask for money and that you can choose not to participate at the conclusion of our session.

Often in life there is a gap between where we are [present situation] and where we would like to be [desired situation]. I would like to discuss this concept with you today, in order to get your thoughts on how we can make this project a success.

Ask the participants to refer to the handout that's shown here in Figure 5.1.

Then ask the following questions:

As you consider the possibility of participating, what fears do you harbor? (present situation)

What would you need to know before you would be comfortable conducting any visit? (desired situation)

You will notice that the answers usually fall within the two failure factors (reluctance to call and fear of failure). Tell the participants that you will answer their concerns before they leave.

Next discuss how to arrive at the "desired" position.

Typical Questions That Volunteers Ask

Who Should Be Interviewed?

Volunteers will call on between five and fifty of the organization's best friends. These will have already been identified in earlier sessions.

FIGURE 5.1

Getting from the Present to the Desired Situation

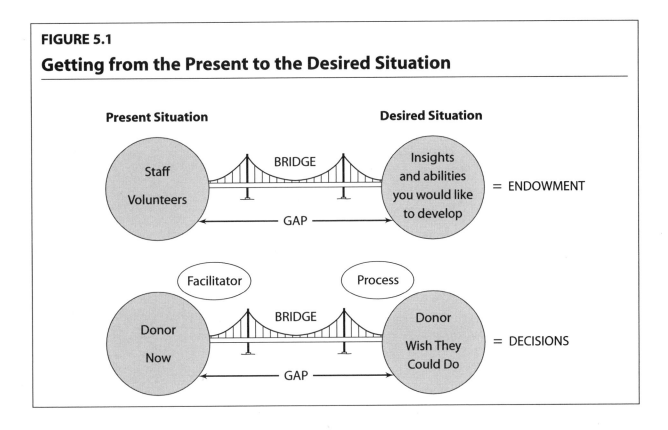

How Do I Respond to the Question, "Why Are You Here?"

The interviewee will have received the Letter of Invitation to Interviewees, which explains the importance of the project. The project will be referred to by a particular project name, such as Pilot Research Project, Listening Project, or whatever name fits your organization. The volunteer might simply refer to this letter, asking whether or not it has been received. If not, the volunteer should produce a copy.

What Do I Say to the Prospect?

Reassure volunteers that they will have a script telling them what to say to prospects. Tell them they will practice this script in several role-play exercises before they leave the meeting. Distribute the script (Worksheet 5.2) at this time.

Here are two key ideas regarding questioning and listening during the interview:

- Direct questions can be considered invasive or prying.

- Indirect, open-ended questions that do not flag a specific answer are superior to closed-ended questions.

WORKSHEET 5.2

Sample Interview Script

PILOT RESEARCH PROJECT

For a telephone debriefing immediately after the interview call: _____

Name of interviewee: _____

Date of visit: _____

Place and time of visit: _____

Interviewer: _____

Instructions to interviewer:

Introduce yourself and share a bit about your involvement and enthusiasm for the organization. Please make all notes directly on this questionnaire—don't worry about neatness. All information you provide us will be held in strict confidence. Feel free to use the back of sheets for additional notes.

All instructions to you will be presented within these bold boxes. *Do not read these instructions to the interviewee.*

A. INTRODUCTION (read to interviewee)

We really appreciate your willingness to participate in this visit. When we need help, it's important that we go to our best friends and ask them what they think. I will listen carefully to what you have to say today. Your answers will be noted and held in strict confidence. As a result of this visit, you may have questions or requests; please be assured that I am eager to address these before I leave. Also, if anything else surfaces during our visit that should be addressed, I promise to follow through.

We have selected you for this visit because of the strong commitment you have demonstrated to the organization, as measured by your comments, involvement, and generous support over the years. Thank you for that support. We really appreciate it.

As the letter of invitation you received noted, you will not be asked for money during this interview.

The purpose of this visit is to learn how our friends feel about the organization and to determine if there is any correlation between how these friends feel about the organization and the way they make decisions with respect to the distribution of their resources.

I'm going to read the questions word for word to maintain consistency in the project and so I don't forget anything. Please be absolutely candid in your response to each question. If you feel uncomfortable with any of the questions, please feel free to decline commenting.

B. RELATIONSHIP WITH THE ORGANIZATION

1. What was your first exposure to the organization?

2. Has your extended family (mother, aunts, father, uncles, siblings, or other relatives) been involved with the organization?   Yes _____   No _____

3. Tell me more.

4. When and how did you first become involved with the organization?

5. What has provided you with the greatest satisfaction since you became involved with the organization?

6. Did any special activity or event bring you a particular satisfaction?

7. Have you developed any special friendships since you became involved?

   Who? _____ Closest friend _____

8. Do you think they feel the same way about the organization that you do?

9. What activities or programs have you become involved in over the years?

Instructions to interviewer:

Wait for an answer. Do not read the list to follow but be alert for mentions of [insert here a list of the various programs, services, and activities of the organization].

How often? _____

Why? _____

In what capacity? _____

How long did you participate? _____

How did this involvement affect your feelings about the organization? _____

10. If you had to do it all over again, would you still choose to be so actively involved?

11. Did a local faith community have anything to do with your introduction to the organization?

    Yes ____   No ____   Which community? _____

    Where over the years? _____

    [Optional] Are you still active in this community?   Yes ____   No ____

    If yes, how long have you been involved there? _____

12. In what ways do you feel the organization has:

    Changed over the years? _____

    Remained the same? _____

13. What have you observed that the organization does better than other organizations?

14. What has motivated you to be so [select appropriate term: supportive, active, generous] to the organization over the years?

15. Is there an area of special interest for you at the organization?   Yes ____   No ____

Instructions to interviewer:

If the answer is yes, respond as follows: "Please tell me more" or "Can you expand on that?"

C. INFLUENCE OF FAMILY OF ORIGIN

1. How would you describe your parents?

2. Did one parent have a greater influence on you than the other?

3. How would you describe this influence?

4. In what ways do you carry their influence with you today?

D. FAMILY SITUATION

1. Tell me about the rest of your family.

2. Do they live in this area?

3. Do you see them often? Do you hear from them often?

4. How are they doing?

5. What do they do for a living?

6. Have there been any recent changes in your family's situation?

7. As you look back over recent years, what effect did your connections with the organization have on your family?

8. As you reflect on your own personal values, what do you feel is the most important value or principle that you want to pass on to future generations?

E. EDUCATIONAL, PROFESSIONAL, VOCATIONAL INVOLVEMENTS

1. How would you describe your educational experience?
   [Optional] Did you graduate?   Yes _____   No _____
   Did you continue your education as an adult?   Yes _____   No _____

2. Tell me about your career path.

3. What was (or is) your spouse's occupation or career path?

4. What occupation, business, or profession were your parents involved in?

5. Were (or are) you active as a volunteer in any other not-for-profit organizations?

6. As you reflect on your early life, did any one person or event influence you greatly?
   Yes _____   No _____
   If the answer is yes, say, "Please tell me more."

F. CORRELATIONAL MATERIAL

Instructions to interviewer:

Feel free to share some of your personal feelings about the organization, your family, parents, and so on, that relate to what has been shared so far in the visit. *Then read the following:*

You will receive a formal report of this research project within sixty days. It will cover the participants' overall reactions to these interviews—their feelings about the organization, about their families, and about their values. How we make decisions about the distribution of our resources is directly related to our feelings about family and values.

   The questions that follow are the heart of this research project. Do our feelings for the organization have any influence on how we want to distribute our resources?

Instructions to interviewer:

Keep it light. Follow the script closely. Then read the following:

G. DECISIONS

I need to ask you a series of eight questions—all concerning what you (and your spouse) might want to do with your available resources.

1. Studies show that a broad cross-section of the population has difficulty making decisions about what to do with their lifetime accumulations. For instance, 70 percent of the population die without a will. Of those 30 percent who have wills, many either don't remember exactly what their will says or don't really like what it says. In other words, *studies show that 7 out of 10 people do not like their current plan.*
   Do you have any thoughts about why, for some people, these decisions are difficult?

2. This question requires only a yes or no response. Do you have a good idea of the amount of your annual income from all sources?   Yes _____   No _____

3. Once again, the question requires only a yes or no response. Do you have a good idea of the amount of your net worth?   Yes _____   No _____

4. [Optional] Once again, this question requires only a yes or no response. Do you have a good idea of the average percentage of total return on your invested assets over the last five years?
   Yes _____   No _____
   Please keep these dollar figures in mind as I move on to the remaining questions.

5. As you think about your loved ones or heirs and what you might do for them, is there an upper limit to how much you want to leave them?

Instructions to interviewer:

After you have listened to the response, mark the most appropriate response.

Interviewee	**Spouse**
a. ____ **No to upper limit**	a. ____ **No to upper limit**
b. ____ **Yes to upper limit**	b. ____ **Yes to upper limit**
c. ____ **Never thought about it**	c. ____ **Never thought about it**

Instructions to interviewer:

Before asking the next question, pick an appropriate amount between $100,000 and $1 million (or more) that represents the interviewee's socioeconomic situation. Do not ask the interviewee to give a figure. Fill in your chosen amount in questions 6 and 7. (*Note:* Please read the handout "How to Estimate Net Worth"; it will help you determine an amount.)

6. If you were to leave *each* of your heirs $ _____ in cash, what do you think they would do with it?

Interviewee	**Spouse**
a. ____ Use wisely	a. ____ Use wisely
b. ____ Misuse	b. ____ Misuse
c. ____ Not sure	c. ____ Not sure

7. If you were to leave them $ _____ , would you want them to receive it all at once?

Interviewee	Spouse
a. ____ Yes to all at once	**a.** ____ Yes to all at once
b. ____ No to all at once	**b.** ____ No to all at once
c. ____ Not sure	**c.** ____ Not sure

8a. If, after providing adequately for yourself and those you are responsible for, you had at your disposal a sum of money that would give you an opportunity to build your own personal charitable dream, what would that dream look like?

Instructions to interviewer:

If the friend does not understand the "dream" question, the following rephrasing is suggested. Make careful notes on the details of the identified dream or charitable project.

8b. If, after providing adequately for yourself and those you care for, there was some money left over that you could use to create your own charitable project, what would you want that project to accomplish?

Instructions to interviewer: **Circle the most appropriate evaluation of their responses.**

Dream cannot be defined   **Dream directly related to the organization**

Dream can be defined   **Dream indirectly related to the organization**

No relationship to the organization

H. INTERPRETATION OF WHAT YOU'VE HEARD

Instructions to interviewer:

You may feel overloaded at this point by all the information you have received from the words, meanings, feelings, and inferences behind the answers to these questions. Most interviewees will have revealed how they feel about the organization and how those feelings affect what they want to do with their financial resources.

Interviewees are usually very direct, but sometimes they share their desires and decisions by innuendo. If you have listened carefully, with understanding, he or she has most likely given you instructions on what to say next.

You should be able to identify those instructions as one of the following impressions. Circle the phrase that best describes your impression of the correlation between their feelings for the organization and the way they make decisions with respect to their resources:

Interviewee:	**Outstanding**	**Good**	**Fair**	**Sparse**
Spouse:	**Outstanding**	**Good**	**Fair**	**Sparse**

Circle one of the five possible outcomes:

Interviewee:	**Done it**	**Intend to**	**Strong might**	**Weak might**	**No interest**
Spouse:	**Done it**	**Intend to**	**Strong might**	**Weak might**	**No interest**

> **Instructions to interviewer:**
>
> **Make no attempt to alter your feedback from what you have heard to what you would like to have heard. Be candid.**
>
> **You should be able to make your summary response in less than five minutes from memory. Read, review, and share in your own words what you have heard. Then read the following to the interviewee:**

You will recall the letter you received from [name of sender]. It stated that the purpose of this visit was to learn what people think about the organization and to determine if there is any correlation between the way our friends feel about the organization and the way they make decisions with respect to the distribution of their financial resources. I repeated this statement on the first page of this survey format.

If I've listened carefully, this is what you've shared with me during our time together. I'll try to be as specific as possible.

> **Instructions to interviewer:**
>
> **You will have been listening for the following cues:**
>
> - **Their feelings about the organization**
> - **Feelings about their family**
> - **Their values and how they intertwine with the organization**
> - **Their thoughts on why, for some, estate planning decisions are difficult**
> - **Their awareness of their income, net worth, and total return on their resources**
> - **Their answer to "upper limit," "do with it," and "all at once" questions**
> - **Their response to the charitable dream question**
> - **Your impression of their estate distribution situation if shared**
> - **Their additional, important information**

1. Is there a correlation between how you feel about the organization and how you want to distribute your resources? Based upon what you've shared with me this is how I would measure the correlation.
   [Choose: Outstanding, Good, Fair, or Sparse.]

2. Also, if I've listened carefully, this is my impression of your present situation:
   [Choose: Done it, Intend to, Strong might, Weak might, or No interest.]

3. Did I listen accurately?

I. THE USE OF DIRECT QUESTIONS TO DETERMINE THE EXTENT OF INTEREST

> **Instructions to interviewer:**
>
> **Do not use the following questions if the rank was Fair or Sparse, only if it was Outstanding or Good.**

In view of what you've shared today about your feelings for the organization, may I ask you some additional questions?

1. If you could, would you be willing to do more?   Yes _____   No _____

2. What would you have in mind? [Wait for a thorough answer, then continue.]

Instructions to interviewer:

Refer to the person the interviewee mentioned earlier who had a significant influence on his or her life.

---

3. Have you ever thought of creating a memorial endowment for that special person you mentioned to me earlier in our visit?   Yes _____   No _____

J. CLOSING

1. Do you have any additional messages that you would like me to pass on to the organization?

For example, here are two ways of asking the same question:

"Do you have a family?" (closed, distasteful, crude, overly personal)

"Tell me about your family." (open ended)

Show volunteer interviewers how to encourage a prospect to elaborate. When the conversation begins to sound as though the interviewee is touching on something important, the volunteer should encourage the prospect to say more about the subject. Open-ended comments like these are preferred:

"Tell me more."

"Would you be comfortable expanding on that?"

"Why do you think that is so?"

How Do I Interpret the Responses?

Explain to participants that they will begin to understand the meaning of the responses they hear before they leave the meeting. They should expect their ability to interpret the responses to improve with each interview. Also the volunteers should understand that they will be coached on what needs to happen next, so they will feel comfortable with the process.

One approach that volunteers can use when preparing to talk to interviewees is to assume that interviewees also have a present and a desired situation. In terms of their financial decisions, there is almost always a gap between where prospects are presently and where they would like to be. The visit helps them progress toward their desired situation. The volunteer becomes a facilitator in making this happen. Any new or amended decision on the distribution of financial resources could very well mean contributing additional resources to the favorite charity. Why? Because these high-affinity individuals are the organization's closest friends. The highest-affinity individuals were ranked in the affinity meeting, so the organization knows who they are.

How to Conduct Role Plays During the Meeting

Allow about thirty to forty-five minutes for the role plays. Give the volunteers a copy of the Interviewee Evaluation Form (Worksheet 5.3), and Helpful Hints for Interviewers (Exhibit 5.5). After the role plays conclude, begin the feedback session, using the instructions included on the interview form. Limit your comments to further maximize audience participation.

WORKSHEET 5.3

Interviewee Evaluation Form

PILOT RESEARCH PROJECT

I was pleased to participate   ___ Yes ___ No

The interviewer was:

    Courteous   ___ Yes ___ No

    Sensitive   ___ Yes ___ No

    A good listener   ___ Yes ___ No

    Patient   ___ Yes ___ No

Participating in the survey helped me:

    Surface the desire to find a way to endow my
    SAVE interests   ___ Yes ___ No

    Address important issues concerning my feelings for SAVE   ___ Yes ___ No

    Reconsider how I want to benefit my family   ___ Yes ___ No

    Rethink what I want to do for SAVE   ___ Yes ___ No

Name _____   Date _____

We welcome your additional observations and comments:

_____

_____

_____

Optional

Please provide me with more specific information on how I can:

___ Prevent funds I want the organization to receive from being eaten up by long-term health or nursing home expenses.

___ Increase my guaranteed lifetime income by making a gift in exchange for a gift annuity.

___ Learn more about benefiting _____ in a manner consistent with my other objectives.

___ Obtain proper legal language or wording to assist my attorney, broker, trust banker or insurance agent in updating my will or other estate distribution planning.

___ Create a memorial endowment as a tribute to someone who had a significant influence on my life.

___ Avoid federal (and state if applicable) capital gains taxes when I sell appreciated stocks, bonds, real estate, or a business.

___ Reduce estate shrinkage.

___ Other.

_____

_____

EXHIBIT 5.5

Helpful Hints for Interviewers

If your prospect prefers not to visit in his or her residence, suggest meeting at another reasonably private location such as a restaurant or coffee shop.

Upon arriving at the interview, try to avoid extended small talk that would interfere with starting the interview. If so enticed, you may say, "Would it be possible for me to [visit your garden, see your workshop, enjoy that pie] after we've completed our interview?" The interview will generate such warm feelings that whatever activities follow will be more enjoyable and take less time. But before you go, if you're not nervous, you're not normal!

Remember This:

- You will not be asking for money.

- You do not have to write down everything you hear—just jot down the main points.

- The letter that was sent to these carefully selected friends stated that the research survey would concern itself with decisions related to their resources.

- The interview form repeated this statement.

- The prospect agreed to participate.

> Remind the volunteers about the four important things to do (and not do) in an interview: (1) thank the prospect; (2) tell the prospect how important he or she is to the organization; (3) keep quiet, listen, and don't editorialize; and (4) do not think about or allude to money.

Instruct the volunteers to tell their interviewees about their own reasons for joining the organization and possibly share their family situation briefly.

Show volunteers how to listen actively to their prospects. Prospects' answers to questions will help volunteers unlock the emotional as well as rational reasons behind the prospects' charitable giving. This will make it possible to design special giving opportunities that will help them achieve their charitable wishes. In fact, the prospects may design it themselves.

How to Discuss the Role Plays

When the role plays are finished, ask the audience what they heard during the role-play visit. What did the prospect say that was meaningful? What was implied? What is the potential meaning for the organization? Some prospects may indicate an interest in making an estate gift; some may alert the interviewers to their commitment to enhancing a specific program or service of the organization. Note these messages.

The volunteers may ask, "Why is the interview so structured?" The answer is that there is a reason for every question. Certain questions purposefully follow others. In the actual interview, volunteers must not skip a question unless it has already been answered. *For example, never, under any circumstances, should questions G1–8 be skipped.* The prospect has an option to pass on these questions (they rarely do), but the interview is not considered complete unless they are asked.

Encourage further audience participation. What messages were missed? Direct this question repeatedly to each of the sections: client, family, vocational, correlation, and decision sections. Each section provides pieces of the information-retrieval puzzle. For example, in the vocational section, the volunteer may learn that the individual has a close relative with a successful business that could be a resource for future contributions. In the family section, it may come out that the prospect's grandmother had a great influence on her life, signifying a potential memorial contribution. Or the volunteer may discover that the individual's charitable dream includes the work of the charity and that the prospect has no heirs.

Distribute the Interviewee Evaluation Form at the conclusion of each role-play exercise. This reminds the volunteers that they will distribute that same form to each prospect at the end of the interview. Show them the postage-paid envelope that will accompany the form.

This form reinforces the prospect's desires and attitudes toward the non-profit and seeks to further define how he or she would like to make better estate-planning decisions. Most interviewees continue to think about the subject after the interview has been completed. The form is a confidential vehicle that enables the organization to obtain other information that may not have surfaced during the interview.

Explain the pre- and post-visit support and debriefing sessions. These sessions ensure that the volunteers understand the interview procedures as well as the interview form.

The support staff should remind volunteers to make a pre-visit reminder call to the prospect and to arrange for a specific debriefing time to visit with the staff support person immediately following the interview. During this post-visit call, the volunteer and staff review the key points of the interview so that a substantive and confidential report can be prepared.

How to Select Prospects

Do not ask for a show of hands as to who would like to participate. Simply proceed to the next part of the meeting: prospect selection. Distribute the list of prospective interview candidates. By scanning the audience you will know who wants to participate and who does not. Generally, 90 percent of those attending the meeting will agree to participate in visiting the closest friends of the charity.

After the meeting, approach those who chose not to participate and thank them for coming. Assure them that you understand why they are not participating and that another volunteer may be visiting with them later because they have been identified as high-affinity friends. Volunteers who want to continue then select the prospects they wish to visit.

Working from a list of contact information labels, ask each volunteer to choose five names. This number is necessary in order to complete a total of three visits, as some prospects will be unreachable. Record the names chosen by each volunteer.

How to Adjourn

Use an assumptive close, that is, a close that *assumes* that individuals will want to participate. The leader simply states what will follow and informs the volunteers about the next meeting—the report meeting. The report meeting should be scheduled for approximately five weeks after the orientation meeting. Instruct attendees to put the date on their calendars. Remind volunteers that they should return the interview form for each of their visits immediately after the telephone conversation with the debriefing support person.

How to Prepare the Report

It is important that the results of all visits be compiled into a report for the subsequent *report meeting*. Delegate this job to an individual who has good analytical skills and attention to detail. This support person will communicate by telephone with all volunteers who have made visits. He or she will then compile the results of the visits into a report. The report format should follow the suggested question list on the Sample Interview Script.

Chapter 6

Understanding and Responding to Donors

DURING THE INTERVIEW prospects often disclose much private information about their personal life and financial resources. Volunteer interviewers will learn about the quality of the relationships in the prospect's family and will probably gain a rough understanding of the financial resources that the prospect may be willing to contribute. This valuable knowledge allows the organization to target the prospect, when appropriate, for one or more types of giving.

In this chapter we show how to summarize the results of visits with top prospects. The report meeting often builds the interest and excitement of volunteers and staff, as they begin to understand their role in involving others in the organization's work.

Of primary importance is that volunteers and staff learn whether prospects will become *qualified* prospects or whether they lack sufficient interest or motivation and should be dropped from the prospect pool entirely.

How to Prepare for the Report Meeting

Volunteers should fill in any incomplete details on their prospect interview forms shortly after (within hours of) their first visit to an interviewee. Before the visit, the support person and the interviewer would have agreed on a time to debrief. Upon completion of the visit, the support person can get an accurate picture of what happened during the visit and ensure that all is recorded in both text and data format. A sample of the final individual report appears in Exhibit 6.1. It may be shortened or lengthened according to your organization's needs.

EXHIBIT 6.1

Sample Prospect Report

Name: Duane and Marcie Roberts
Organization: Church of the Apostle
Interview #11

Interview conducted by Al Markus on December 11, 1999

Descriptive adjectives: She is warm and sensitive. He is hospitable and insightful. He is in his late 60s. They have lived like they speak. They grab on to issues and get involved. They do what they say.

Feelings and experiences with Church of the Apostle: They were invited to join when they moved into this neighborhood in 1954. They have been active since that time. Presently he is cochair of the capital campaign, and they have made a significant commitment.

Greatest satisfaction: Duane replied, "theology, preaching and worship." For Marcie it is people, the sense of community, and the expression of faith.

Greatest need: For him it is seeing the gospel preached. For her it is friendships.

Changed or remained the same: Church of the Apostle is a more open place than in past; however, it still has a sense of caring and community.

Does better: The church engages itself with the social issues of the day in word and action.

Motivation: For her it is doing good things with money. For him it is a responsibility for service and charity.

Special interest: The continuing work and study of Christian theology. For her it is Bible study. He would complete the building program that would allow the implementation of programs and community. They have raised $.5 million in the last 6 months.

Quotes: One pastor had a great influence on him on "race relations" that was critical to his thinking process.
Staff really appreciated: All in their own unique way.

Family relationships, education, and occupations: His parents were indifferent to church. Mother was a reader with a strong intellect and an inquiring mind. She had the greater influence on him. His dad was a skilled worker. Marcie's parents were involved in a small business in rural community. Had ties to the church. Mom had a greater influence.

Children: Five sons, all doing well. Three are teachers, one a social worker; the youngest is a senior at Union Seminary. All are married. They are day care providers for one grandchild on a regular basis.

Career paths: She was trained as a teacher, taught; once the family arrived she became a homemaker. He spent time as a political consultant and ended his career as an executive with a corporate foundation. Earlier he was a reporter, spent time with the university and was on the governor's staff.

Education: Graduate work at the university

Charitable interests, other: Answered no but actually he is heavily involved with 4–5 outside charities that are supported and integrated into the outreach programs of the local faith community. Two of these are Peace Academy for the public schools—a second chance for teens in chemical dependency—and Hospitality Network for homeless people.

Greatest influence: A female professor at Moorhead State Teacher's College. She provided a profound influence in guiding his perspective on the world.

Eight Key Questions

1. 70/30 response: Duane responded most people don't do long-term planning; they fear running out of money.
2. Knowledge of total income: Yes
3. Knowledge of net worth: Yes
4. Knowledge of five-year total return on invested assets: Yes
5. Upper limit: Yes, by implication. The question surprised them! They felt they would "have nothing left because they would give it all away." Amount used: $500K.
6. What would children do with it: Use wisely
7. Would they want them to have the $500K "all at once": Yes; however, Marcie kidded that she doesn't think the money would last because one spouse might lose it in an investment venture.
8. Dream: He replied to make a difference in people's lives: people, poverty, and help those that face great challenges in their lives. She replied for the church in education and service.

Additional Information

1. Correlation to local church: *Outstanding*
2. Action or intention at this present time for local church: *Strong Might*
3. Willing to do more: He would give more so that the church could serve others.
4. Final comments: He believes that faith communities should hold a broad definition of stewardship and that stewardship should be a natural part of worship and action.

Action Plans

1. Long-term implications of the interview will play out in their personal and church lives.
2. The evaluation form opened the door to "providing for future generations."
3. The attached Memo to File might be a useful tool to stimulate prompt follow-through and give a picture of how their charitable objectives could be implemented in separate and appropriate legal documents to assist their faith community. The fund might honor their mothers, who had a great influence for each of the prospects.
4. Because of Marcie's comments about her son's wife, it might be valuable to introduce the Charitable Income Stream illustration.
5. Evaluation form: They checked off Yes to a desire to find a way to continue their giving to future generations [endowment implication] and yes to the "visit helped me address important issues concerning my feeling for their faith community."

Debriefing staff: John T. Smith

The support person then ranks the interviewers from 1–14 (from outstanding to poor) and ranks the three individual volunteer interviews that were most indicative of prospect involvement and interest from 1 to 3.

The individual prospect report should contain the following items:

- An extensive text summary of the prospect's feelings for the charity
- An extensive text summary pertaining to the prospect's family
- A database representation, if possible (see Exhibit 6.2) listing other responses or interpretations, either check-offs or in text (see Exhibit 6.3)
- A list of responses from the prospect's evaluation form (see Exhibit 6.2)
- Recommendations for follow-up, based on the data gleaned
- Outline of a tentative action plan

How to Package the Reports

Provide copies of the individual reports for each interviewer. Also provide summary report copies of the Volunteer and Staff Evaluation Form (Exhibit 6.3).

What to Expect from the Meeting

The volunteer interviewers should leave the meeting convinced that they are the best people to take responsibility for what needs to be done, both in follow-up actions and in visits with prospects.

Other expectations are that the volunteers will participate in developing the action plan discussed during the session. The meeting should encourage volunteer and staff ownership of the project.

The volunteer and staff interviewers will reveal how they applied their involvement to their own personal philanthropy (see Exhibit 6.3).

How to Conduct the Meeting

Distribute the agenda that appears in Exhibit 6.4.

Next distribute the individual prospect reports to their respective interviewers.

Interviewers Share Experiences

It is best to have the most effective interviewers begin by sharing their best interviews, keeping the names confidential. These volunteers may have discovered at least one or two prospects who have already made or want to make an estate gift. They have good news to share.

Ask the volunteer to share in his or her own words what happened in order of the structured sections of the interview form. By the end of the time allotted, all core volunteers should have shared their interview experiences.

The leader or support person should supplement the discussion as necessary to improve understanding.

Interpreting Critical Information

The following will help the leader explain how to interpret the information. Note that certain patterns develop consistently during the interview. For example, a profile of the best estate or transfer-of-wealth donors or volunteers often looks like this:

- They frequently rank high on their affinity for the charity.
- They always answer yes to the "upper limit" question.
- Their charitable dream is directly related to the charity.
- They get an Outstanding ranking on the correlation of their feelings for the nonprofit to the distribution of their estate.

A profile of the best campaign donors or volunteers often looks like this:

- They rank high on their affinity feelings for the charity.
- The correlation of feelings to distribution of estate is rated Sparse or Weak.
- Their present estate distribution system would be described as Weak Might or No Interest.
- They are vague about their charitable dream or want to fund the dream with cash flow rather than estate resources.
- They answer no to the "upper limit" question (they want their heirs to have all of their financial resources).
- They don't want heirs to receive funds all at once (they create trusts).
- They have a strong sense of community responsibility.
- They have had extensive campaign experience.
- They create foundations and use community foundations.
- They are gifting to heirs during their lifetime.

Remember that the volunteer interviewer promised to share the results of the visits with the prospect. Because confidentiality has been promised, the volunteer is the ideal person to make the follow-up visit. The results of the visits may be shared by mail, but in-person sharing opens up a chance to have a second in-depth conversation.

EXHIBIT 6.2

Database Representation of Prospect Responses

09/28/2000   **Interview:**

Org.   04/01/2000 - 12/31/2002

Date _____	**Age** _____
Category _____	**Project** Residential Alzheimer's Cottage
Status _____	**Address** _____
Interviewer _____	**City/State/Zip** _____
Responses _____	**Spouse** _____
	Debriefer _____
	Upper Limit Amount _____

< Client History >

☐ ~Alzheimer Concerns
☐ ~Bequest-Potential
☐ ~Leadership Role - Past or Present
☐ ~Multiple Family Connections
☐ ~Multiple Generations Served
☐ ~Staff Connections
☐ ~Visit(s) Facilities - Frequently
☐ Events: Multiple
☐ Events: Never Misses
☐ Resident: Current
☐ Resident: Friend
☐ Resident: Parent
☐ Resident: Potential Future
☐ Resident: Relative
☐ Resident: Sibling
☐ Resident: Spouse
☐ Volunteer Involvement: Auxiliary
☐ Volunteer Involvement: Heavy
☐ Volunteer Involvement: Light
☐ Volunteer Involvement: Medium
☐ ~Volunteer Involvement: None

< Evaluation Responses >

☐ Returned: Possibility Future Giving-Endowment
☐ Returned: Reconsider Family Benefit
☐ Returned: Requested Information
☐ Returned: Rethink What I Want to Do - PRC

< Family/Personal History >

☐ ~Farm/Agricultural Roots
☐ ~Foundations - Create and Use
☐ ~Gifting to Heirs
☐ ~Grandchild's Education Concern
☐ ~No Apparent Heirs
☐ ~No Family
☐ ~Pioneer Spirit & Pride
☐ ~Spouse Equally Supportive
☐ ~Trusts in Place for Heirs

☐ ~Widow - Widower - Single
☐ Heirs Financial Situation: Doing Well
☐ Heirs Financial Situation: Have Need
☐ Heirs Financial Situation: Some Not Doing Well
☐ Parents: Generous Givers
☐ Parents: Influenced Life
☐ Relationships: Fair
☐ Relationships: Good
☐ Relationships: Great
☐ Relationships: Mixed
☐ Relationships: Poor
☐ Share Interest in Organization: Mixed
☐ Share Interest in Organization: No
☐ Share Interest in Organization: Yes
☐ Socio-Economic: Affluent
☐ Socio-Economic: Comfortable
☐ Socio-Economic: Influential
☐ Socio-Economic: Modest
☐ Socio-Economic: Self Made

☐ Volunteers/Other: Many
☐ Volunteers/Other: None
☐ Volunteers/Other: Select

< Interpretation >

☐ ~Campaign/Project Prospect
☐ ~Campaign Experience - Extensive
☐ ~Community Asset
☐ ~Confidence-Financial Integrity
☐ ~Desires to Help Needy Residents
☐ ~Faith Motivation - Strong
☐ ~Gift Annuity Candidate
☐ ~Life Income/Trust Criteria
☐ ~Memorials - Interest - Potential
☐ ~Not Satisfied - Present Plans
☐ ~Person of Great Influence
☐ ~Resources Available to Give
☐ ~Tax - Shrinkage Concerns
☐ ~Values Related to Mission
☐ ~Wants to Be Used

- [ ] ~Willing to Do More
- [ ] Affinity to Mission: High
- [ ] Affinity to Mission: Low
- [ ] Affinity to Mission: Medium
- [ ] Annual Giving: Only Interest
- [ ] Annual Giving: Only Opportunity
- [ ] Annual Giving: Sprinkled Widely
- [ ] Estate Gift: Done It
- [ ] Estate Gift: Intends to
- [ ] Estate Gift: Might - Strong
- [ ] Estate Gift: Might - Weak
- [ ] Estate Gift: No Interest
- [ ] Feelings Distribution: Fair
- [ ] Feelings Distribution: Good

- [ ] Feelings Distribution: Outstanding
- [ ] Feelings Distribution: Sparse
- [ ] Volunteer Candidate: Campaign
- [ ] Volunteer Candidate: Interviewer
- [ ] Volunteer Candidate: Other

< Prospect Responses >

- [ ] All At Once: No
- [ ] All At Once: Not Sure
- [ ] All At Once: Yes
- [ ] Do With It: Don't Care
- [ ] Do With It: Misuse
- [ ] Do With It: Not Sure
- [ ] Do With It: Use Wisely

- [ ] Dream: Can't Be Defined
- [ ] Dream: Education Related
- [ ] Dream: Faith Community - Local
- [ ] Dream: Never Thought
- [ ] Dream: Not-For-Profits - Faith Related
- [ ] Dream: Not-For-Profits - Other
- [ ] Dream: PRC - Directly
- [ ] Dream: PRC - Indirectly
- [ ] Financial Awareness: Income
- [ ] Financial Awareness: Net Worth
- [ ] Financial Awareness: Total Return
- [ ] Upper Limit: Never Thought
- [ ] Upper Limit: No
- [ ] Upper Limit: Yes

Text Responses

Client History

Does Better _____

Feelings for & History with Client _____

Special Interest _____

Family/Personal History _____

Feelings for & History of Family _____

Greatest Influence _____

Values to Pass On _____

Interpretation

Evaluation Form Comments _____

Final Messages _____

Recommended Action _____

Prospect Responses

Dreams _____

Motivation _____

Non-Client Dreams _____

Opinion 70/30 _____

Willing to Do More Example _____

EXHIBIT 6.3

Volunteer and Staff Evaluation Form

Note: The following sample form contains a summary of actual responses from a library.

1. Did your participation in this research project change or modify your own thinking in regard to the distribution of your personal resources?

   Yes   9   No   4

   (Quote from the form) "Several years ago my husband and I had discussed bequests to the library."

2. If yes, when did this process start?

   Training session   5   Reading on subject matter   1   Discussion with spouse ___

   Reflection   5   Discussion with another ___   During actual interviews   2

3. Do you want the library to benefit?

   Yes   6   Maybe   6   No   1

4. Have you considered increasing the level of your estate giving as a result of this project?

   Yes   5   No   7

5. Do you see any benefit in spreading out bequests to your heirs over a number of years? (charitable income stream application)

   Yes   7   Maybe   2   No   1

6. Will you use some of the knowledge gained in this project when you upgrade your legal documents?

   Yes   4   No   2   Possibly   8

7. What specifically?
   a. In the future, not yet.
   b. To re-check on legal advice we have already received.
   c. I don't have a will. I have got to get one in place. As a single mom it's very important for me to have one.
   d. That a percentage of the growth of assets is an appropriate gift.
   (*Note:* as estate grows, donate some of the growth.)

8. Do you intend to update your estate planning documents?

   Yes, soon ___   In the next 6 months   4   No urgency   9   Recently did this ___

9. Do you have an attorney in whom you have confidence?

   Yes   10   No   4   Unsure ___

10. Is there anything you would like to share that would be helpful to a volunteer-driven endowment building program?

    Immediate dollars in the coffer are not the major issue. (*Note:* the volunteer feels that current needs are not urgent; what the organization needs is ongoing endowment fund to perpetuate specific programs and services.)

11. What did you like about the program?
    a. Positive experience confirmed belief in depth of support for library.
    b. The structure, the way it was handled, and our two great teachers!
    c. New insight into the importance of listening.
    d. Personal contact with friends and colleagues.
    e. Good introduction to the concepts of effective fundraising.
    f. The people.
    g. Interviewing concept.

12. What didn't you like about the program?
    a. Lingering problem in integrity, as intent is ultimately a donation.
    (*Note:* The staff person continues to be concerned about manipulation. The only person raising the issue. However, this is an indication that this staff member is not a leadership person.)
    b. I used my own time, as had to come back evenings and weekends to work on daily responsibilities.
    c. Not efficient use of time. Changing dates of meetings a disaster.
    (*Note:* The library changed set calendar, which caused great inconvenience for this busy physician.)
    d. Nothing.
    e. Time consuming (but worth it).

EXHIBIT 6.4

Sample Report Meeting Agenda

9:30 A.M.	Welcome and Overview (Good News; Findings)	CEO
9:45 A.M.	Review and Reading of Individual Reports	All Participants
9:55 A.M.	Sharing of Visiting Experiences	All Participants
10:30 A.M.	Break	
10:40 A.M.	Continued Sharing of Visiting Experiences	All Participants
11:35 A.M.	Implication of Responses	
11:45 A.M.	Advice and Recommendations	All Participants
Noon	Lunch and Continued Discussion	All Participants
12:30 P.M.	Personal Evaluation Opportunity	Volunteers and Staff
1:00 P.M.	Adjournment	CEO

Need for Training in Tax or Legal Areas

During the report meeting, volunteers and staff may indicate that they don't know enough about estate planning. They do not need to know estate law, nor should they attempt to practice law. However, they can help the prospects prepare for their personal consultations with their legal and tax counselors.

Many questions on the interview form raise issues that address concerns or objectives that might preclude leaving bequests or dollars outright to heirs. Also the prospect may request additional information about estate planning on the evaluation form. Some concerns that may arise include

- Heirs wouldn't or might not use funds wisely.

- Interviewee doesn't want or isn't sure about leaving heirs funds all at once.

- "How are they doing?" question reveals family difficulties.

- Interviewee wants to provide educational funds for children or grand-children.

The volunteers only need to know about the two methods that any individual can use to leave money to heirs: (1) make an outright bequest (heirs receive the principal) or (2) leave income or interest to the heir rather than the principal. Share the following examples with the volunteers.

Outright Bequest Versus Twenty-Year Term Trust

If $100,000 (or any amount) is placed into a reserve account for five, ten, or more years, this account generates income to be distributed to the heir for the period specified. At the end of the period, the corpus or remaining principal may be given to the next generation or charity, as specified by the donor (see Figure 6.1).

Here's how the income stream option works: $100,000 is invested for a total return of 10 percent and a payout of 8 percent. (The corpus or principal will grow by 2 percent every year.)

Assume that a "dream charity" benefits after twenty years. Heirs would get $160,000 spread over twenty years. The charity would get $214,000 at the end of twenty years. The donor would thereby distribute a total of $374,000 (174 percent more) than if he or she had made an outright bequest of $100,000 to heirs.

The individual has two choices: (1) leave heirs money outright at death or (2) leave heirs an income stream at death.

Prospects might make the following observation: "All you are doing is using the interest to pay the bequest." This is true. Thus the great majority

FIGURE 6.1

Charitable Income Stream: Trusts

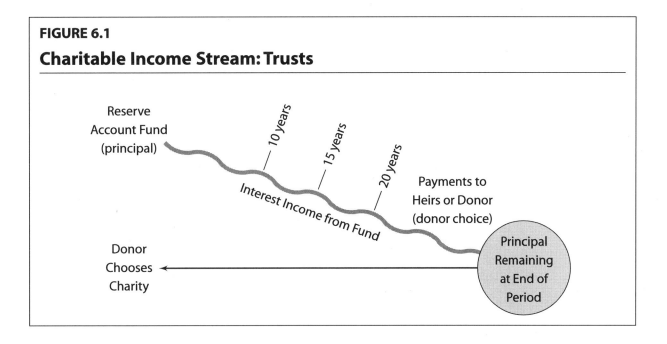

of prospects will opt for an income stream bequest. They believe that they are protecting an heir while still gifting a bonus to their beloved charity. That way they can make their dollars valuable to both parties. Note that no one from the organization (staff or volunteers) should presume to provide tax or legal advice. Their role is simply to create opportunities to facilitate decision making for prospects and donors.

Many who are not highly motivated toward charitable giving will give the corpus (remaining balance in the trust) to their favorite charity at the end of the life of the trust. They don't mind giving the principal away if the trust accomplishes and addresses their other objectives.

Memorial Endowment Funds

Many questions on the interview form signal a possible interest in honoring a special person. Some of these are

- A person had a significant influence on the interviewee's life.

- A sibling, parent, or child is deceased.

- A sibling left the interviewee money.

- A loved one has been affected by an organization's mission.

- A loved one was cared for by a nursing home or hospice, for which the interviewee is grateful.

- Three or more generations have been involved in a faith community or children's nonprofit.

- No heirs are living.

How to Use the Memoranda to File

The Memoranda to File (Worksheet 6.1) can be used to help the prospect clarify his or her intentions. We suggest that you have several versions of this document. The need becomes apparent after reading specific individual reports. This tool is never discussed with the volunteer interviewer during the orientation meeting or in the debriefing exercise with the support person. The volunteers and staff are most receptive to the value of this tool after hearing the powerful messages provided by prospects during the visit.

Often the volunteer will agree to become a facilitator by using the Memoranda to File to help a charitable friend accomplish a stated goal. Some volunteers will also want to use these tools in their own estate planning.

How to Do Follow-Up Coaching

Follow-up coaching is suggested for subsequent visits to prospects with an interest in estate-type giving.

Questions to Use in Follow-Up

In retrospect, what did you think of the interview? Was it helpful? In what way?

When the organization receives your bequest, what would you like done with your money?

Have you ever thought of connecting your gift to paying tribute to your father or mother's influence on your life and their passion for learning and books?

Would you be willing to consider underwriting the overhead costs connected with the use of your collection (appropriate if the bequest is a product or materials)?

Let me show you a draft of a memorial to the named individual. Is it helpful? What would you want to change?

Could I tell you about the income stream for heirs?

Another suggestion is to deliver the written material or legal language requested on a prospect's mailed-in evaluation form personally. This material should not be mailed; delivering it opens another opportunity to help. Don't miss it! When the prospect comes to the organization, ask when you can set up an appointment.

During this visit suggest that the spouse might enjoy visiting with the executive or other appropriate individual to talk about what he or she

WORKSHEET 6.1

Memoranda to File

Note: This example can be used as a model and adjusted to fit the circumstances. The purpose of it is to give prospective donors a substantive way to think about making a memorial gift.

The Roberts Family Endowment Fund

The Roberts Family Endowment Fund has been established by the testamentary planning and possible lifetime contributions of Marie and Duane Roberts in gratitude for the theology, preaching, worship, friendships, sense of community, and expressions of faith they have experienced at the Church of the Apostle.

It is their desire to pass on what they have received to future generations. They also want to pay tribute to their mothers, May Sherring Schultz and Harriet Cole Roberts, for their inquiring minds and lasting influence on their lives.

This fund shall be established as a permanent endowment and maintained by the [*insert choices on which organization would manage, invest, and distribute the income from the fund*], and the income only shall be used for the following purposes:

One-third for maintenance and/or building needs that would encourage the implementation of programs and community

One-third for educational programs and/or service

One-third for helping those who face great challenges in their lives

The fund administrators shall keep in mind the objectives of the donors and tastefully connect the name of the fund with this perpetual distribution.

During their lifetime, the donors retain the right to revoke or amend this memorandum.

February ____ , 2000

_____
Marie Sherring Roberts, Donor

_____
Duane C. Roberts, Donor

would like to see happen. The volunteer could say something like, "There is someone I think would be helpful to you. She has helped me in my planning, and I feel certain you would like her. Would that be helpful?"

How to Confirm the Prospect's Intentions

When there is other strong evidence that the prospect wants to include the charity in his or her estate planning, it will be evident by the end of the interview. The interviewer confirms this assumption by restating his or her understanding of the prospect's intentions: "Am I correct in thinking that the correlation between your feelings for the charity and the distribution of your resources is outstanding?" (*Note:* This language is taken directly from the interview form.) This essential step minimizes the likelihood that the interviewer will misinterpret the prospect's intentions. It also provides an additional signal to indicate the seriousness of the prospect's interest in philanthropy.

Distribute the confidential Volunteer and Staff Evaluation Form (Exhibit 6.3). This form provides a way for volunteers to indicate their personal philanthropic interests.

Cover Letter and Project Report

Finally, an example of a project report (Exhibit 6.5) and its accompanying cover letter (Worksheet 6.2) will show you how to craft your own documents.

The project will energize your natural leaders. Individuals who participate in the report meeting are very enthusiastic about their experiences. The most important thing you can do is to convene a follow-up meeting as soon as possible to help them plan and implement their fundraising objectives.

• • •

We have now completed the initial cycle of affinity fundraising and are ready for your core volunteers to develop the plans and implement the projects that they believe are most beneficial for the organization.

WORKSHEET 6.2

Cover Letter for Final Project Report

Date _____

Dear _____ :

The Final Report of the Pilot Research Project is enclosed. You will recall that we made a commitment to send everyone who participated in the interviews a formal summary of what we learned from your collective responses.

The main purpose of this study was to assess our potential for participating in the campaign. A secondary purpose was to find a way to build a permanent endowment to serve future generations of students and faculty.

To accomplish these objectives we first needed to find out how our friends feel about the Library. The next step was to determine the extent of the correlation between these feelings and the way participants want to make decisions with respect to the distribution of their resources. The interviews provided encouraging evidence that this correlation is strong.

Your participation has provided us with great insights that we are still digesting. I hope you will see yourself in the report. The project confirmed that listening to our friends and making personal visits are the best ways to communicate.

We are very encouraged by the findings because they give evidence that you and others you represent are willing to help us meet the challenges of tomorrow.

I welcome your comments and observations after you have read the report.

Sincerely,

[Name] _____

[Name of library] _____

EXHIBIT 6.5
Final Project Report

LIBRARY: FINAL REPORT

Pilot Research Project on Resource Decision Making

We want to express special appreciation to the following volunteers and professional staff who gave of their time to conduct forty interviews with strong friends of the Library during September and October 1999.

Their visits were enjoyable and instructive for the future of the Library. The commitment they demonstrated made this report possible. [Insert list of interviewers.]

The following report is representative of the observations, feelings, and information that you shared during the interviews. We are grateful for your willingness to share so much of yourself and your feelings for the Library.

Reactions to the Interview: Summary Data

We are happy to report that in forty interviews we learned the following information from your evaluation forms and direct statements, and from our professional interpretation of your comments:

- When asked, you willingly shared how you felt about the Library, as well as the extent of the correlation between these feelings and the way you make decisions with respect to the distribution of your resources.

- The thirteen professional staff and two volunteers who conducted the interviews attempted to measure the correlation between your feelings for the Library and how you make decisions with respect to the distribution of your resources. They evaluated the correlation as follows:

    18 percent had an Outstanding correlation.
    26 percent had a Good correlation.
    28 percent had a Fair correlation.
    28 percent had a Sparse correlation.

- What you have already done or may do for the Library in any future estate plan was evaluated as follows:

    15 percent have Already Done [something for the Library].
    3 percent Intend to Do [something for the Library].
    27 percent indicated a Strong Might.
    32 percent indicated a Weak Might.
    23 percent indicated No Interest.

- Statistics relating to the charitable dream or a charitable project:

    64 percent of those participating were able to define a personal charitable dream.
    21 percent identified the Library as directly embodying their charitable dream.
    21 percent identified the Library as indirectly embodying their charitable dream.

- Statistics relating to the thirty-one (two unsigned) evaluation forms that were returned directly to the project manager:

    100 percent indicated they were pleased to participate.
    23 percent indicated a desire to find a way to endow their special interests at the Library.

∫ 64 percent indicated that participating helped them address important issues concerning the Library.

15 percent indicated that participating helped them reconsider how they wanted to benefit their family.

36 percent indicated that participating helped them rethink what they wanted to do for the Library.

18 percent requested specific information on resolving issues they were wrestling with.

- Statistics relating to the distribution of assets or transfer of wealth:

  36 percent indicated there was an upper limit to the sum they wanted to leave heirs.

  46 percent indicated that there was no upper limit to the sum they wanted to leave heirs.

  13 percent indicated that they had never thought about an upper limit for heirs.

  62 percent indicated that heirs would use their inheritance wisely.

  23 percent were not sure their heirs would use their inheritance wisely.

  10 percent indicated that their heirs would not use their inheritance wisely.

  64 percent want their heirs to receive funds all at once.

  18 percent did not want their heirs to receive funds all at once.

  15 percent were not sure about leaving their heirs funds all at once.

  15 percent revealed criteria or interest in a memorial endowment for a loved one.

  15 percent revealed or indicated a need to pursue trust income for certain heirs.

  30 percent were clearly not satisfied with their present planning documents.

The consensus reached was that the majority of those interviewed are still in the process of making decisions relating to the distribution of their financial resources.

The project revealed an encouraging correlation between how friends feel about the Library and how they desire to make decisions with respect to the distribution of their resources.

Feelings About the Library

General comments:

The best in the nation.

Let's get serious about libraries.

For a state institution, it takes its mission seriously.

Since the age of nine, libraries have been my home.

There is a need for people to value the work of librarians.

Comments related to funding needs:

There is an untapped reservoir of support at this Library.

The Library should actively solicit the personal collections of retiring faculty.

I want to see my money used to buy an extra journal that they couldn't otherwise buy.

I believe the Library needs a $20 million endowment for its collections.

I am passionate about the Library being the heart of the institution.

The Library is going in the right direction. Ten years ago, there were no giving options.

I might give my collection of Japanese books once they move into the new building.

My reasons for giving today are different than they were twenty-five years ago; today I am more aware of needs and feelings of responsibility. I also have more money.

EXHIBIT 6.5
Final Project Report, continued

Comments on what the Library does better than other libraries:

The qualified and intellectually alert staff.

The scholarly journals. The quality of the collections.

More service hours than Gray Memorial Library and best employee attitude.

The events they put on, such as Book Week, Awards Day, and Tea and Treasure Day.

It does just about everything; it is bigger than the Harvard or MIT Math Libraries.

Comments on motivation for supporting the Library:

The Library is fundamental to every discipline.

I see the importance of donating to take care of the materials.

The Library is the critical indicator of the strength of the community.

I appreciate the research help the Library gives me and others.

The Library is the most important tool after pencil and paper to do the work of my profession.

I am prejudiced for libraries because we could not buy any books; we borrowed them.

Books have always been important to me.

Charitable Dream or Project

For some, the idea of a personal charitable dream or project was a new concept. For many others it was relatively easy to share what they would want to create through a bequest, living trust, or other estate distribution vehicle.

Often it was difficult to ascertain whether dreams for education, learning, books, or academia extended to or included the mission of the Library.

Library-Related Plans

Comments on plans for Library gifts:

To will books to the Library

To endow the Philology Program

To give money to support the Library, specifically the History Collection

To provide funds for the maintenance of the collections

To use own money to make donation (husband not philanthropically inclined)

To will a donation to the Children's Collection

Part Three

Affinity Fundraising in Action

Chapter 7

Campaigns and Special Projects

IN CHAPTER SIX, where we described the report meeting, we discussed the characteristics of capital campaign donors. You may wish to review this information. It will prove to be of significant value when it is time to identify leaders and prospects for a campaign.

With support and guidance, your core volunteers will develop a fundraising plan for capital and special projects. Some organizations use a listening-research project like the one we've described as an alternative to the more traditional feasibility study, which seeks to determine whether adequate resources are available to complete the project.

This chapter describes two case studies in which affinity fundraising fostered the success of capital and special project campaigns. One is a project for an arts organization in a small town. Many believe that it is difficult to raise money in small towns. Nonetheless, this organization was successful because of the efforts of its board and other high-affinity volunteers.

The second case study shows how you can set an example by using big-gift donors to bring other large donors to the giving table. Although it was basically a rural campaign, this example also shows that location is not critical when raising money.

CASE EXAMPLE: SMALL-TOWN CAPITAL CAMPAIGN

At the time it launched its building campaign, the art studio, Artstart, was just a small program with a budget of $60,000. Located in the town of Beaumont, Texas, Artstart had a good reputation within the small community. They provided studio space, exhibition opportunities, educational programs, and community outreach for people in southeast Texas and southwest Louisiana. The organization was also responsible for presenting ten visual arts exhibitions and twelve musical concerts each year.

Despite its small size and budget, Artstart was a high-affinity organization. The organization served a broad constituency. Youth enjoyed workshops in pottery or clay. School districts, state-run care institutions, local mental health care programs and safe houses, as well as at-risk youth programs, all worked with the organization to foster the notion that art is an important part of everyday life.

It was a fun campaign from the beginning, as many volunteers stepped up to help. A local advertising firm provided two volunteers, who assisted with media relations and publicity. The executive director involved the ten-person board—individuals from all sectors of the community, including teachers, lawyers, and journalists. The board members secured support from their friends. The key project starters—two Mobil Oil employees—were able to use their $5,000 gifts to leverage another 2-to-1 match from their company. Another foundation contributed a sizeable gift.

Local artists donated artistic designs, and the two individuals from the advertising firm launched a promotion plan that would center on T-shirt sales and "buying a square foot of art." Many became involved in donating a square foot of art. At the end of three years, the Artstart volunteers and staff had raised $130,000 in new money and obtained gifts from some five hundred contributors.

Cultivate Big-Gift Donors First

Making your big-gift or estate-gift donors your first priority for other types of giving opportunities is the most cost-effective use of your resources. Why? It's a bigger pot of money. Most important, once a friend decides to make a big gift, all other decisions relating to giving out of income become trivial in comparison.

When it is financially possible, the majority of estate donors would prefer to help sooner rather than later. Think of it this way: if your largest donors have already reserved a significant sum of money for your organization for future delivery, wouldn't it be wise to think of them as potential leaders and prospects for a campaign?

Consider the next case example. It illustrates how to involve high-affinity individuals in volunteer opportunities. The example also indicates that your donors will offer gifts naturally when you listen to their ideas and concerns.

CASE EXAMPLE: A UNIVERSITY CAMPAIGN

As planned giving director for the University of Minnesota, John Ryan had organized a seminar for the nonprofit legal, accounting, insurance, and financial planning community. A luncheon speaker was needed. Ryan wanted to find someone who could represent all of the communities. Helen Henton came to mind.

But why Helen? She was an active farm manager and a 1925 graduate of the university's law school. She had a trust relationship with a major bank for over twenty-five years. She was both a farm manager and owner of a regionwide industry. Although a very private person, she was also an articulate supporter of education and philanthropy. She appeared to be the perfect motivational speaker. Of course, Helen accepted the challenge and was the hit of the seminar.

Sometime later, Ryan invited Helen and ten other $1 million estate donors to a luncheon. The purpose of the invitation was to find out whether the donors would like to participate on the advisory committee for a proposed recognition group called the Heritage Society. What all invitees had in common was that each had planned to leave his or her entire estate (more than $1 million) to various University of Minnesota programs.

The meeting was a tremendous success, as the donors applauded the proposed society. Later that day on the drive home, Helen Henton quietly but with intensity said: "John, I want you to know that today's meeting was the most important meeting that has ever taken place at the university. I haven't definitely decided, but there is a possibility that I may have $50,000 to give away this year (commodity prices were up). Do you have any thoughts on what this $50,000 might be used for?"

Of course I did! Here was the package I presented to Helen for the $50,000 gift: Helen would commit $50,000 for a campaign to raise $200,000 for Agriculture Merit Scholar grants to attract outstanding students to the College of Agriculture. The college would then find twenty to forty lead givers throughout the state to match Helen's $50,000. These donors would commit $1,000 to $5,000 each. The $50,000 raised from this group would be added to Helen's gift, bringing the total to $100,000. The College of Agriculture would then go statewide and raise another $100,000 from the Friends of Agriculture community. The total leveraged would be $150,000, and the total raised would be $200,000.

The following year Helen made the offer again. That year we suggested four departments or programs that had great fundraising potential. All needed a boost to jump-start their development program; in this respect they were similar to small charities. None had an established fundraising program with a dedicated staff. They might be perceived to be low affinity, although they were actually high affinity because all had a group of high-affinity friends who were likely prospects.

Three departments were given $10,000 matches, and the fourth was given a $20,000 match. All were to leverage 3 to 1 on the gift. One program didn't make it because they never got off the dime. No mercy was shown because they showed they didn't take the match seriously. Their failure opened up a match opportunity for another department.

Helen's legacy continues. Even though she died in the mid-1980s, her influence continues to this day. Starting at point zero in 1984, the Agriculture Merit Scholar fund, which is now called the Dean's Scholar Endowment, is worth $2,013,490. As this text goes to print, another dollar-for-dollar match to create an Agriculture Futures Fund totaling $1 million is under way.

Helen had offered the same $50,000, 3-to-1 match offer to another nonprofit organization. She gave away a total of $100,000 during the last two years of her life and leveraged another $300,000 for a total of $400,000. She knew how to make things happen.

• • •

You will discover the generosity of big-gift donors who choose to participate in multiple giving opportunities. Your volunteers will be excited to be a part of this process—one that brings resources to the organization. Encourage them to follow up on the opportunities provided in their interview reports and to make a specific plan for the cultivation and solicitation of each individual.

Chapter 8

The Annual Fund

IT IS IMPORTANT for all nonprofit organizations to convert prospects into donors and to continually build greater levels of affinity for the organization. This chapter will provide ideas for how to find new people who may have affinity for your cause. You will learn how to encourage these new prospects to become regular annual donors and eventually big-gift donors.

Let's begin with a case study that shows how a small group of high-affinity people began leveraging lump-sum gifts to their organization and thus grew from a zero-income group into one that grossed $900,000 in its eighth year of operation.

Note that wherever you identify affinity, you identify possibilities for your organization. Even organizations with modest beginnings, such as the one in the following example, need not wait to begin experiencing phenomenal results.

CASE EXAMPLE: HOW AN ANNUAL FUND GREW

SAVE (Suicide Awareness/Voices of Education)—a suicide prevention agency—was able to find high-affinity friends who helped build the organization. They all shared a common experience: depression that, in some cases, ended in suicide.

The History of SAVE

Andy and Alice had just lost their beautiful daughter to suicide. Although they longed for support, at the time there was no community of survivors; consequently, no support groups were available to them.

In August 1989 a committee of six survivors was formed. They held their first event in April of 1991; 150 people attended. The conviction grew that they could build a group of advocates. In October 1991 they formed a board of directors.

Andy, Alice, and others on the early committee of six wrote out personal checks to pay operating expenses. Andy and Alice functioned as the executive leadership for the small group. The annual fund began to grow as survivors and their friends sent in checks.

By 1996 a husband and wife who were friends of Andy and Alice made a gift of $5,000 to pay for a billboard that would increase the visibility of the organization. Sometime later, the donor's wife asked Alice if she planned to remain involved in the organization. After discovering that Alice was indeed committed to the mission, the donor's wife sent a check for $50,000.

The next year Alice and Andy informed their major donor that they felt it was time to hire an executive director. The donor's advice was that SAVE needed start-up funding for three years rather than one. He asked Andy to draw up a business plan and budget. Andy produced this overnight.

These personal, donor friends committed $50,000 for each of three years as an unrestricted gift to the annual fund and an additional $200,000 for each of three years if the organization could secure a match. The commitments would total $750,000; every kind of gift would count against the match.

Alice believes that another event motivated these generous provisions: the donor husband's closest personal friend had recently committed suicide.

The following shows the revenue growth that SAVE experienced:

Year 1: Organization begins with the first board of directors.

Years 2–4: Donors support the organization with personal checks.

Year 5: $67,000 in total revenue

Year 6: $167,000 in total revenue

Year 7: $500,000 in total revenue

Year 8: $900,000 in total revenue

The daughter's death created affinity; the friend's death increased the level of affinity. Almost everyone connected with the SAVE organization has been either a survivor or has had first-hand, family experience with depression.

No matter where you are in fundraising efforts, you can benefit by involving big-gift donors in your project. A lump-sum contribution from a donor can leverage additional revenues when used as a match or campaign incentive. Many donors will match gifts on a 4-to-1, 3-to-1, or 2-to-1 basis. Based on what you have learned thus far, who, among your high-affinity donors, might want to help you with an annual gift campaign?

How to Target Specific Groups

For all organizations at all levels of maturity, marketing strategies are especially important for your development program. For example, it is critical that marketing communications be directed to organizational stakeholders in a way that is appropriate to their interest and level of involvement. For this reason many organizations divide their database into distinct segments, or interest groups.

Although these segments differ for every organization, some common ones are religious organizations, school faculties, university staff, professional associations, corporations, foundations, fraternal societies, and small businesses. You may wish to segment the file based on how recently donors contributed.

Managers of today's individual giving programs know how important it is to provide different communications to each of the various donor segments. Effective targeting of segments encourages the development of communications that will build affinity—communications that are closely aligned with the interests, income, and lifestyle of the prospects.

An effective method of developing segment-specific communications is to delegate the management of the solicitations for each segment to a manager. This serves several purposes. First, a division of labor allows for more effective management of the job. Second, it allows a politically (or otherwise) correct appointment of a candidate who has a special relationship or affinity with a particular group.

A faith community might be one group that demonstrates affinity for the work of your organization. For example, a retired rabbi might have many contacts within the Jewish community. As manager of the solicitation function for religious institutions, the rabbi could seek new gifts from religious groups or individuals, as well as renewal gifts from the organization's donors who are classified as part of the "religious group" segment.

How Volunteers Can Cultivate an Affinity Group

The first task is to identify who group members might be, where they might be found, and how they can be attracted to the organization. Then you, or one or two volunteers, can formulate a focus concept, as well as ideas for activities that will keep prospects connected to the organization.

Create a social group for friends. The YMCA case example later in the chapter illustrates how this can be done. Part of their strategy was to involve senior groups and create a comfortable environment for them. What constituencies have a natural affinity for your organization? Consider the following: students of high school or college age, postgraduate professionals, professional groups, seniors, males, females, young marrieds with small children, service clubs, and career centers.

Two of the largest-growing demographic groups that are now entering philanthropy are youth and seniors. Don't overlook the possibilitites with these groups. Even youth of high school age are starting foundations and having events to raise money for nonprofit organizations.

Call a meeting to ask what activities they enjoy and what times of day are good for attendance. You may start small but as friends invite friends your group will grow. If you give people an opportunity to socialize with others, they will develop plans to help the organization they love. The organization will begin to feel like home to them.

For example, a library could cultivate several age groups: seniors, youth, singles, and married couples. You may even mix groups based on interests as long as there is, in fact, some common interest. For example, if you want to raise money for a technology-media collection, you might wish to cultivate local groups or professional associations that focus on these topics. Professional computer and technology users' groups would be candidates.

Allow these groups a time to meet every month by providing a socializing opportunity. Bring in guest speakers on topics of interest, as well as other professionals they could network with. Most important is to keep a mailing list of all who attend. Meet the educational, social, and professional needs of the groups, and they will appreciate your organization. Educate these individuals about how their work is a match for the mission of your organization. The individuals with the greatest affinity will increase their involvement over time.

Orienting Volunteers to a Project

Whenever possible, establish a project's financial goal together with the volunteers. The goal may be based on the prior year's results, as well as the amount of time and resources available for the task. If volunteers will be visiting or making telemarketing calls only with cold prospects who know little about the organization, their job will be much harder. A prospect must usually learn much about an organization and how it does its business before making a gift.

During the goal-setting discussions, establish a realistic timeline for the project. Next, establish the requirements for all communications, whether they will be by telephone or in person, or will use some other format. Volunteers must be aware of the proper protocols: Must the nonprofit manager approve the way a volunteer communicates? Is there a restriction against telemarketing? Must certain colors or styles be used in printed material?

Orient volunteers to the staff that they will need to work with. These individuals may include, for example, the executive director, program staff, or the database manager. This will help volunteers access organizational information and alert staff to be receptive to future calls from the volunteers.

Inform the volunteers of what resources are available, including possible sources for in-kind support. Ask the volunteers to track their results using the Donor-Prospect Results Form shown in Table 8.1. Arrange for periodic checkpoints throughout the solicitation period.

Recognize the volunteer manager once the job is completed. A debriefing with the individual will inform you of the arrangement's flaws and advantages, as well as whether the volunteer will continue.

Delegating Tasks to Volunteers

In addition to working with targeted segments or members of an affinity group, consider delegating the following tasks to volunteers:

- Cultivate ten current donors throughout the year.

- Manage the lapsed high-end donor communications (donors who give larger gifts but have not given for one year or more).

- Devise strategies that secure resources and improve renewal rates for donors from year to year.

- Identify and cultivate twenty new corporate or business prospects throughout the year.

- Develop and produce a newsletter for corporate donors, individual donors, or memorial donors (ideal for a business with resources for printing or with staff capable of producing and publishing copy, such as a graphic arts school or electronic publishing firm).

- Develop a strategy for securing e-mail addresses of interested donors, as well as an on-line newsletter or bulletin to keep them abreast of organizational developments. Devise periodic solicitation strategies to be implemented on-line.

TABLE 8.1

Donor-Prospect Results Form

Organization	Contact Name and Phone Number	Gift Range	Interests	Dates and Times	Strategy
Retirees from the Smith Corporation	Sally Peterson (206-890-3456)	$500–$3,000	Likes kid projects (kidstart program); in-city only	1st Monday month	100 in group; bring envelopes; 15-minute speech only
ABC Business Systems	Sam Proward, director of marketing (349-987-9078)	$50–$150	Interests of CEO; likes environmental	Call in morning best	Speak to marketing managers; 10 minutes; intro/questions
Chambord International	Eliot Yound, director of human resources (209-999-0000)	$1,000+	Gives to rural areas; event sponsors; golf tournament?	Fall of the year	Work with development

The ideas are endless. They can be simpler than the ones in this chapter. Or they can be more complex if the volunteers have multiple talents and resources. Develop your own list based on the unique talents of your volunteers. Meet with them individually and ask how they believe their talents can best be used, or consider developing a task group.

How Volunteers Can Be Successful Speakers

Many organizations set up a speakers bureau; that way volunteer speakers can promote the organization's mission and help identify potential high-affinity individuals. It's a job that is highly rewarding for the volunteer as well as the organization.

Consider the following when setting up a speakers bureau. Make sure that the volunteer speaker has ample information about the organization and can use the information to design a specific speech for each audience. Be ready to suggest topics or strategies. For example, a corporate retiree might want to know how a former employer is involved in the community or how other retirees and survivors are working to help the organization.

Inform your volunteer speaker about the key strategies and financial needs of your organization. If it is not possible to directly solicit gifts, the speaker may be able to set the stage for later development activities such as volunteer recruitment or subsequent fundraising mailings.

Some groups allow the direct solicitation of audiences; others prefer to send a letter of solicitation after the engagement that outlines the need for the gift. Instruct your volunteer to ask about the requirements of each engagement. He or she will need to obtain the protocol and the contact name, as well as a suggested gift "ask." The speaker should ask about the range of gift amounts, as well as the possibility of asking for a major gift that may cover a specific organizational need.

Another way to assist the volunteer is to provide a sample solicitation letter (Exhibit 8.1). With this guidance, volunteers may then write their own letters, making adjustments to them as needed for each audience.

Some organizations secure as much as 30 percent of their organizational budget through speaking arrangements, obtaining new gifts at every engagement. You will generate higher response rates by providing a reply device and envelope. This allows the individual, group, or entity to make a gift immediately following the presentation or up to several weeks afterward. Although somewhat more expensive than other types, a *bangtail* envelope may be used. This is a one-piece, printed communication that combines the brochure with an envelope. Depending on the type of engagement, the speaker

EXHIBIT 8.1

Sample Solicitation Letter

Dear [prospect's name]:

Thank you for speaking with me last week about your organization's interest in helping nonprofit organizations that serve children.

Every year the Children's Agency serves some 1,100 children between the ages of five and nine at sites at various schools and organizations throughout the city.

Many of these children are homeless. In addition to their need for food and shelter, they often lack basic health services and personal health care items. Our organization provides toothbrushes, hairbrushes, nail clippers, and other necessary items for personal hygiene. Local corporations donate many of these items.

We have more than one hundred volunteers who work some two thousand hours yearly with the children on homework, tutoring, and general recreation. This is where we have the greatest need. Basic school supplies are needed, as well as calculators and other learning aids. At a cost of $3.00 per child, we need approximately $3,000 yearly for this budget item alone.

Clearly, we must help these children succeed in school if they are ever to better their situation in life. If your organization could help us with a gift of $2,000, we would greatly appreciate it. We have a vendor that would donate pencils. We will be happy to print the name of your organization on the pencils if you so desire.

I have enclosed a copy of our charitable organization tax registration and a copy of our annual report.

Thank you again for your interest in our organization.

Sincerely,

[Volunteer's name]
[Name of agency]

P.S. Enclosed is a story about one of our children. I hope you find it interesting. It shows how vital your support is!

may be able to directly solicit individuals in the audience by providing the bangtail, or a contact person may be supplied with a solicitation letter. The advantage of this system is that the essential pieces are less likely to be lost.

If you have more than one volunteer speaker, you may wish to assign groups or suggest that they work as a team to avoid duplication. Locate leads from your local chamber of commerce and from the Yellow Pages® in the phone book.

Possible engagements might include

- Corporate retiree luncheons

- Local sorority and fraternity functions

- Consulting group meetings, for example for accountants, lawyers, or financial advisers

- Service clubs such as the scouts; civic clubs like Kiwanis and Lions Club

- Religious gatherings

How to Use Telemarketing Effectively

Some organizations feel that caller ID, call blocking, and answering services hamper their ability to make telephone contact with donors. Although these factors may challenge the telemarketing effort, we contend that telemarketing remains an extremely effective tool for nonprofits to use in cultivating affinity. It is an underused marketing tool, considering the benefits that accrue from the telemarketing effort. Perhaps most important is that it provides a personalized method for an organization to communicate with an individual prospect or donor. Such highly personalized contact encourages maximum benefits in our depersonalized society.

Some organizations use a mature solicitor to telephone prospects for estate gifts. The solicitor asks the prospects a series of questions that will be used to determine the likelihood that the prospect will make a transfer-of-wealth gift. Many of these questions can be found in the interview script in Chapter Five. Or you may develop your own telemarketing staff, either volunteer or paid. This has distinct advantages. For this reason we will provide you with guidelines on how you might launch such an effort later in the chapter.

First, let's consider a YMCA (Young Men's Christian Association)—an organization that effectively organizes its senior constituencies and involves them in a telemarketing effort. This effort not only provides human resources for the YMCA but it serves to build affinity within this important segment.

The following example shows how an organization can involve volunteers or members in a fundraising campaign. As you read this example, note that throughout the campaign, the YMCA was able to achieve its fundraising goal and still meet the needs of its volunteers. They creatively involved their loyal followers in ways that maintained their interest, met their personal timetables, and matched their desire for socializing, community service, and fun.

Any organization with a moderate-size membership or dedicated following can replicate this success. This includes schools, groups such as political and art groups, and other membership organizations. Adapt the techniques we describe in the YMCA example to the unique culture and mission of your organization.

An indicator of the success of the YMCA's campaign is that, in a recent year, approximately $50,000–$55,000 was raised; expenses were approximately $6,000.

CASE EXAMPLE: A TELEMARKETING CAMPAIGN

The Southdale YMCA, which serves the suburban areas of Minneapolis, Minnesota, implements an annual, volunteer-centered telemarketing program.

Recruitment

Months before the campaign begins, a press release to a local newspaper outlines the campaign, its goals, and the need for volunteers. At the same time, an internal recruitment program obtains the personal commitment of key staff and a small number of key volunteers who agree to participate in the project.

During training and orientation, staff members explain the need for the campaign, including a description of what the funds will support. Volunteers learn that fundraising solicitation by phone is pressure-free. They can have fun while helping the YMCA promote their story.

Recognizing that senior citizens are an exceptional human resource, the Southdale YMCA cultivates this group throughout the year. Various activities such as field trips and potlucks provide both a recreational and social outlet for seniors. The group perpetuates itself, as friends invite other friends to join. This is one of the primary affinity groups that participates in the phone campaign.

Timeline

An overview of the specific actions the campaign takes looks like this:

Four Months Prior

- *Involve the staff (explain their role in supporting the campaign).*
- *Secure a site for telemarketing (minimum of ten phone lines).*
- *Hold recruitment nights (set up a table every Monday night in the YMCA lobby).*
- *Solicit local businesses for prizes and donations of services, discounts, and products.*

Two Months Prior

- *Print the media announcements.*
- *Send a recruitment postcard to members and senior groups.*
- *Post internal flyers in the building.*
- *Mail 3,000 posters to the member list, requesting volunteers.*

One Week Prior

- *Hold kick-off celebration.*
- *Begin volunteer training.*
- *Begin two-week calling period.*
- *Hold a post-calling, volunteer recognition celebration.*

Administrative Support

One development staff member and six other staff members provide part-time support for the campaign. They participate in volunteer recruitment, promotion, food service, calling, and celebrations.

Two groups of volunteers are recruited: callers and team captains. A team captain is responsible for managing the work of ten people. He or she manages caller recruitment and attendance, as well as their pledge amounts and totals.

Training

Training—given during a sixty- to ninety-minute period—is conducted on the same day the campaign begins. Volunteers are assigned their calling cards, which list pertinent donor information such as name, address, and giving history. They listen to role plays performed by experienced callers and participate in a simulated TV game show that allows them to "guess" the answers to common questions they may hear while on the phone. Food is served.

Calling (6:00–8:30 P.M.)

Fun and frivolity characterize the atmosphere. Callers set their own schedule for the number of nights they will volunteer. They may attend "Italian Night," "Movie Treat Night," or any of a number of different theme nights. Callers are motivated to reach higher pledge goals by gift incentives they may choose at various pledge levels. Food is served, and door prizes are given as calling incentives for early attendance and dollars pledged. Team captains motivate callers for "highest pledge" and "first pledge for the evening."

How to Launch Your Own Telemarketing Campaign

Perhaps by now you have identified a potential source of volunteers. Now is the time to involve your staff. At a minimum, they should know how the proceeds from the campaign would support their programs or budgets. Ask them to choose an activity that would support the campaign. Make a list of possible involvement activities: food, promotion, volunteer recruitment, supervision, and administration are all options. Get their agreement on the dates it will be done, then make a list for yourself as to who will accomplish what.

Recruiting

How many callers will you need? Callers will be able to complete approximately six to eight calls per hour, not including disconnections, hang-ups, and messages on answering machines. To determine the number of calling hours use this formula:

$$2{,}000\ names \div 6\ (calls\ per\ hour) = 333\ calling\ hours$$

From this formula you can calculate the average number of hours each caller will work during the campaign.

Look among your most dedicated volunteers and donors. They may be willing to devote seven or eight days to a calling effort for a short period of time. Post flyers at universities, schools, and employment offices. Some organizations run a block ad in their local newspaper or send press releases to corporate volunteer offices. See Table 8.2 for more specific suggestions.

It is not essential to have prior experience with telemarketing. More important, the caller must not be timid and afraid of rejection.

TABLE 8.2

Where to Recruit Volunteers

Job	Where to Find Volunteers	Vehicles to Attract Volunteers
Database manager	Professional association meetings, churches, corporate volunteer offices, computer training vendors, high schools, technical schools, colleges	Post flyers; send e-mail to professional groups; speak with counselors, pastors, and school placement officers
Web developer	(See database manager), professional Web developers' training associations, Small Business Association, chamber of commerce, computer training groups	Send a volunteer speaker to a conference Web developers attend to talk about the value of volunteer services; meet with corporate placement staff, advertise in newsletters and on cable TV; speak at Rotary, Kiwanis, and other service clubs
Telephone shift supervisor	College placement offices, donors, members, former staff	Talk to placement staff
Telephone calling staff (volunteer or paid)	(See supervisor); interest groups (sororities, fraternities, stock brokerage firms, real estate offices, businesses with a telemarketing department)	Ask business to use phone lines at their site

Determining a Payment Method

If you will use paid callers, the normal wage depends on economic conditions in your locality. A wage structure that works for many is to provide for a minimum hourly wage, plus bonuses.

You may structure bonuses in various ways:

- Highest number of pledges

- Number of pledges received above a certain dollar amount

- Highest dollar amount of pledges for a certain time period

- Highest number of gifts during the hour

When structuring bonuses, remember to offer nonmonetary incentives to callers as well as the opportunity to earn additional revenues. Moreover, bonuses serve to make the evening fun. They add a spark of excitement that everyone should be able to share. These rewards also motivate callers to higher levels of achievement.

However, bonuses should be designed so that the donor relationship is maintained. Quickness of call completion, although important, is not necessary for success. If a caller spends a lot of time on the phone but always seems to bring in larger gifts, you may wish to offer this caller a special bonus.

An evening meal or luncheon is a nice reward for callers. Or provide a piece of fresh pie, a fruit plate, or other small item as one of the bonuses. Secure donated gifts from your business supporters, such as a free lunch, discount coupons, dry cleaning, a limousine ride, or tickets to special events and movies. Publicize the callers' success with flyers, posters, and articles in the organizational newsletter. This is another job to delegate to your volunteers. One volunteer might secure the bonus items, or your telemarketing shift supervisor might do that job.

Although few callers wish to devote every night to a campaign, it is important to assemble a few callers at one time in order to build camaraderie. This will provide time for the shift supervisor to observe their calling habits and provide valuable feedback, and callers will learn much from each other. After this initial period, or toward the end of the campaign, you may wish to allow some callers to complete their calls at home.

Callers should agree to complete a minimum number of shifts, as well as a training session. You may wish to offer several three- to five-hour shifts, both morning and evening, so volunteers can choose three or four days during the week to make calls.

Appointing a Shift Supervisor

A volunteer or staff member who demonstrates leadership qualities would probably be a good shift supervisor. This person monitors caller behavior, provides suggestions for improvement, and charts volunteer hours, as well as completes calls. In general, the supervisor manages the entire project so that you, the development manager or executive, will be able to continue other important duties. Many organizations hire a shift supervisor who is responsible for implementing the entire project, from recruitment to training and shift supervision to gift receipting and accounting.

Meeting the Physical Requirements for Telemarketing

Here is some of what you'll need for a telemarketing effort:

- Six to seven phone lines, at a minimum
- Pledge cards and postage
- Training materials for callers
- Donor or prospect information sheets for callers, including phone number, address, and prior giving history
- Thank-you letters
- Credit card payment options

It is not essential that you have phone numbers for the individuals listed in your database. Several vendors will provide phone numbers for names in a database for a fixed charge per 1,000 names (TELEMATCH at 1-800-523-7346 and Computer Graphics at 623-581-6770). Names and phone numbers can also be ordered from a list broker. Not all lists have phone numbers, but some donor lists have been used for telemarketing purposes. In this case you may wish to order the information to be printed on 3" × 5" cards. This extra charge is well worth it, as it allows you to distribute specific names to each caller.

If you are using the records from your own house file, you may wish to organize it into a format that is useful for the caller. Examples of useful data include

- A ten-year giving history
- Size of gifts
- Date of gifts
- Name, address, phone number

- Age, date of last contact
- Personal notes column ("do not call during dinner hour," "has no children," "friend of staff member")

What type of results can you expect? Results vary, depending on the quality of the list and the organization. Generally, cold prospect lists average a 10 percent response rate, with existing donor lists ranging from 25 to 50 percent. Fulfillment—the number of pledges that are actually collected—generally ranges from 50 to 90 percent.

The use of credit cards is highly encouraged, as it virtually guarantees payment on a pledge. For those without credit cards, you may wish to send a reminder every thirty days until the pledge is collected. It is common to send seven to ten reminders over a six-month period.

Using a Preapproach Letter

We believe that an advance letter notifying donors and prospects that you will be calling offers significant advantages. Usually this sets the stage for a more positive response by phone, and you may receive a gift by mail, making the call unnecessary.

Dealing with Caller ID and Answering Machines

You may wish to experiment, but nonprofit organizations often find that *not* using a block on calls probably helps. In other words, if the prospect knows you are calling, he or she may wish to speak with you. This may be different with individuals who know nothing about your organization. You may even leave a message on their machine and send a pledge card they can fill out. A certain percentage of these cards are always returned with a gift.

Training for Telemarketing

Schedule a three- to five-hour session to discuss the following:

- Use of a pledge chart (a quick reference to help the caller explain gift amounts to the donor)
- Protocol for making the call (see Exhibit 8.2 for a sample script)
- Instructions for adding personal information to the donor's record
- Instructions for completing the pledge card, for both check and credit card
- Expectations about hours (shifts) to be served
- Practice in role playing
- Ways to maintain the donor relationship

EXHIBIT 8.2

Sample Telephone Script

Hello, this is _____

    [Identify yourself.]

I'm calling to thank you for your generous giving over the years.

    [Inform donors how much they gave and when. If the donor has a long history, use summary statements.]

May I ask what interests you about our programs?

    [Refer to the information sheet for results to share with the donor.]

Would you be willing to help us again this year?

Would you consider increasing your commitment?

    [Ask for 25–50 percent more than the prior giving amount, depending on donor's receptiveness.]

    [Repeat donor's agreed upon pledge amount and method of payment.]

Optional

1. Do you have any messages you would like to pass on?

    [Introduce the matching fund challenge for annual giving.]

2. Did you read about the matching fund opportunity? The challenge donor wants to encourage more participation and has challenged us to increase our gifts by 25 percent.

3. The challenge donor wants us to encourage bequests to the school. Consequently, we hope to schedule some wills seminars. Shall we inform you when they are scheduled?

    [Debrief callers to gain valuable information.]

The last item on the list—maintaining a relationship with the donor—is extremely important. Callers should be instructed to respond to donors' wishes at all times, removing them from the list if requested or calling back at an appropriate time.

Provide short summary statements about numbers served and yearly accomplishments. If callers have good information and can speak quickly and knowledgeably, they will generate larger gifts.

Finding Nuggets of Gold

In the training meeting you asked callers to note any important personal or pertinent information on the Donor-Prospect's Record Card. Some donors will tell you about their personal situation; some might be nuggets of gold. For example, you might discover that one of your callers has spoken to an elderly woman or man with no children who loves the organization. This should definitely be noted with a gold star as "investigate for possible visit." Make sure that you brief callers at the start and end of every night so you can be alerted to these possible new, high-affinity donors.

Retaining Volunteers

At the end of each day and at a campaign's conclusion, it is useful to have a debriefing evaluation session to determine the strengths and weaknesses of the project.

At this time it is appropriate to ask each volunteer whether he or she would like to continue in the same capacity next year.

• • •

These are just a few methods for cultivating affinity. When you involve everyone in the organization in cultivating affinity, you shorten your path to success.

Chapter 9

Adapting the Model to Fit Your Organization

YOU MAY BE WONDERING whether there are differences in the way different organizations should proceed with a project like the one we've been describing. The answer is no. Whether your organization has been around a month or fifty years, the technique remains the same. And it does not matter whether your organization is a synagogue, church, or library, or is an arts, health, education, or human services group. Both low- and high-affinity organizations can benefit from affinity fundraising.

The questions on the interview form are designed to encourage prospects to identify their own philanthropic needs and wishes. Many of these questions can be used with individuals who have affinity but may never have given before, or who might have no prior knowledge of the organization. This chapter will provide additional ideas for low-affinity organizations that wish to add more high-affinity people to their organization.

Adaptations for Low-Affinity Organizations

If your organization has only a few high-affinity individuals, we suggest that you begin with this small group and begin expanding your circle. Your plan might be to visit the closest two to five friends, then expand the circle to the next-closest eight to ten friends. The idea is to begin with your inner circle and work outward.

What Questions to Ask

You may wish to use a condensed version of the interview form in Chapter Six. Include the key questions on the form regarding (1) discovering affinity, (2) asking for names of other potential high-affinity friends, and (3) soliciting the advice of high-affinity friends. Then convene informal meetings at which you adapt the techniques we explained in Chapters Four through Seven.

Here is a condensed interview form for low-affinity organizations:

When did you first get involved in our mission?

Why did you get involved?

What motivated your involvement and generosity over the years?

What effect has your involvement had on your life and the life of your family?

Who, in your opinion, cares more about this mission than anyone else you know?

Can I benefit from their insights?

Can I tell them you suggested I visit them?

Who else do you recommend I visit?

What advice do you have for me as I attempt to provide leadership?

What do you think we should do next?

Would you be willing to help?

Tell me about your family. How are they doing?

What influence did your parents have on your life?

Analyze the responses from the individual meetings to determine who among your group can help you. Consider these questions:

Do they have a high-affinity attitude toward the charity?

Are they passionate about the organization?

Do they believe that the organization has the potential to do more?

Do they have a picture of what they would like to achieve?

Drop anyone from the group who shows little interest.

The following questions can help you select natural leaders for the project:

Do they have some ideas about how to get there?

Do they know others who might become involved?

Do they have the interest, talent, and motivation to help?

Who stands out?

Who is the natural leader? You may wish to meet with your most natural leader, or leaders, to take the next step.

How to Expand Your Circle

At this point you may know who you would like to have in your leadership group. You have a good idea who might be your most natural leader. Arrange another visit with that person. Share your findings.

Tell the person about your inner circle of two to five friends. Share the positive, common threads of encouragement that your friends have spoken. You may develop a report that summarizes the answers to questions on page 106.

Tell the person about the eight to ten newly identified friends. Suggest the possibility of calling a meeting of the other four high-affinity friends that are members of the inner circle.

Note the prospective leader's reaction to this information. If it is positive, share the following information and tentative plan.

Invite the three to five most interested (and able) friends to a two-hour lunch. Let them know what you learned from the interviews. Ask them to share with each other how they reacted to your visit and what thoughts they had after the visit. Tell them you have discovered a wider group of new as well as old friends that should be involved. They may be interested to know that volunteers are usually more effective in communicating with prospects than salaried professionals. What you really need is their help and advice.

Ask whether they would be willing to volunteer ten hours during the next four weeks. They would each

- Spend two hours preparing for visits (the orientation meeting)

- Complete three personal visits in about six hours

- Attend a two-hour wrap-up meeting to evaluate the findings (the report meeting)

If each member of this inner circle of friends agrees to help you conduct a Pilot Research Project, you can get internalized research from another twelve of the nonprofit's best friends. Ask what they think of the idea. Would they be willing to help?

• • •

These are just a few suggestions. Adapt the techniques to fit your organization. Remember that both high- and low-affinity organizations will come to understand the full potential of development after the completion of an initial listening and research project.

Now that the interview process has helped you more fully understand the needs and desires of your prospects, you will be able to see whether they fit more naturally into estate, campaign, special project, or annual giving. Your best prospects may want to contribute in more than one area.

Afterword

OUR GOAL was to enhance your skills and increase your enthusiasm for affinity fundraising with volunteers. At this point you are equipped to begin meeting with your high-affinity friends. Even though you will feel apprehensive, soon your apprehension will melt into excitement, as many of your friends respond with enthusiasm and support.

Don't wait. Get started today. It's that simple. Just pick up the phone and call one of your trustees or board members. Meet for lunch and try out some of scripted questions.

Then when you return to the office, make an appointment with your best campaign prospect and your best annual donor. Don't stop when things start to snowball. Just keep going. Soon you will discover that you will have secured the financial support needed for your organization.

Yes, along the way you'll need to evaluate how the process is working. You'll make adjustments so that you and your volunteers can progress in a fashion that best suits the needs of everyone involved.

You'll discover how you can improve your results and enhance relationships with your special friends. Marketing communications of all kinds will help you build interest and excitement.

You will also make sure that the volunteers are getting the support that they need from staff.

After a while, you will discover that your high-affinity friends will probably be calling you to tell you what they'd like to do for your organization. It doesn't get any better than that! We wish you the best and hope that you will arrive at this point soon.